Windows 8.1 & RT 8.1
for the
Older Generation

Jim Gatenby

BERNARD BABANI (publishing) LTD
The Grampians
Shepherds Bush Road
London W6 7NF
England

www.babanibooks.com

Please Note

Although every care has been taken with the production of this book to ensure that all information is correct at the time of writing and that any projects, designs, modifications and/or programs, etc., contained herewith, operate in a correct and safe manner and also that any components specified are normally available in Great Britain, the Publishers and Author do not accept responsibility in any way for the failure (including fault in design) of any project, design, modification or program to work correctly or to cause damage to any equipment that it may be connected to or used in conjunction with, or in respect of any other damage or injury that may be so caused, nor do the Publishers accept responsibility in any way for the failure to obtain specified components.

Notice is also given that if equipment that is still under warranty is modified in any way or used or connected with home-built equipment then that warranty may be void.

First Published – February 2014

British Library Cataloguing in Publication Data:

A catalogue record for this book is available from the British Library

ISBN 978-0-85934-748-8

Cover Design by Gregor Arthur

Printed and bound in Great Britain for Bernard Babani (publishing) Ltd

About this Book

In 2012 Windows 8 and RT introduced a radically different way of operating a Windows PC, based on a new *Start Screen* consisting of an array of *tiles*, as shown on the right. Tiles may be tapped with a finger or clicked with a mouse  to launch *apps* (i.e. programs) or Web sites. Windows 8.1 and RT 8.1 were released in 2013, incorporating changes based on user feedback. **This book covers all versions of Windows 8, 8.1, RT and RT 8.1**, mostly referred to in this book simply as Windows 8.1, since all versions are very similar in appearance and are operated in the same way. Where necessary, any differences between versions of Windows such as Windows 8.1 and Windows RT 8.1 are explained in the text.

The first chapter gives an overview of the new operating systems and some of the pre-installed apps. Next the new *Modern User Interface* is covered. The book then shows how to set up the computer to match your personal preferences, followed by Ease of Access features to accommodate any special needs.

The setting up of an Internet connection is described together with essential Internet security precautions. Finding information, communicating using e-mail and social networking sites like Facebook and Twitter are then explained. Downloading apps from the Windows Store, many of them free, is also covered. Free worldwide telephone calls using Skype are described. The final chapter explains the upgrading of computers running earlier versions of Windows to run Windows 8.1 or RT 8.1. Applications software for Windows 8.1 and RT 8.1 is then discussed.

Jargon is avoided where possible and a Glossary of essential technical terms is included at the end of this book.

About the Author

Jim Gatenby trained as a Chartered Mechanical Engineer and initially worked at Rolls-Royce Ltd using computers in the analysis of jet engine performance. He obtained a Master of Philosophy degree in Mathematical Education by research at Loughborough University of Technology and taught mathematics and computing in school for many years before becoming a full-time author. His most recent teaching posts included Head of Computer Studies. The author has written many books in the fields of educational computing and Microsoft Windows, including many of the titles in the highly successful "Older Generation" series from Bernard Babani (publishing) Ltd.

The author has considerable experience of teaching students of all ages and abilities, in school and in adult education. For several years he successfully taught the well-established CLAIT course and also GCSE Computing and Information Technology.

Trademarks

Microsoft, Windows, Windows XP, Windows Vista, Windows 7, Windows 8, Windows 8 Pro, Windows 8.1, Windows 8.1 Pro, Windows RT, Windows RT 8.1, Surface, Surface Pro, Windows Live Mail, Office, Word, Excel, OneNote, Paint, Skype and Publisher are either trademarks or registered trademarks of Microsoft Corporation. Facebook is a registered trademark of Facebook, Inc. Twitter is a registered trademark of Twitter, Inc. BT is a registered trademark of British Telecommunications plc. Google is a registered trademark of Google, Inc. All other brand and product names used in this book are recognized as trademarks or registered trademarks, of their respective companies.

Acknowledgements

I would like to thank my wife Jill and our son David for their help and support during the preparation of this book. Also Michael Babani for making this project possible.

Contents

1

Introducing Windows 8.1 & RT 8.1 1

What is Windows? 1
The Evolution of Windows 2
Windows 8.1 — The Modern UI 3
Versions of Windows 8.1 4
Upgrading from Windows 8 to Windows 8.1 5
The Microsoft Surface and Surface Pro 6
Viewing All of Your Apps 7
    Windows 8 and RT 7
    Windows 8.1 — the Arrow Button 7
    Windows RT 8.1 8
The Traditional Windows Desktop 8
Using the Desktop in Windows 8.1 9
    Starting Windows 8.1 in the Desktop 9
Go to the Apps Screen Instead of the Start Screen 9
Tiles on the Start Screen 10
    Live Tiles 11
    The Travel App 12
    The Mail App 13
    The People App 13
    The Weather App 13
    The SkyDrive App 14
    Some Utility Apps in Windows 8.1 14

2

Navigating Windows 8.1 15

Introduction 15
Basic Mouse Operations 16
Basic Touch Gestures 17
Launching Apps Using Tiles 18

Returning to the Start Screen from an App   19
   The New Start Button in Windows 8.1   19
   The Start Menu in Windows 8.1   19
Launching an app   20
   Typing the First Few Letters of the App's Name   20
   Using an Icon on the Apps Screen   20
   Pinning a Tile for an App to the Start Screen   20
Switching Apps   21
Displaying Two or More Apps Side by Side   22
The Charms Bar   23
   The Search Charm   23
   Searching in Windows 8 and RT   23
   Searching in Windows 8.1 and RT 8.1   24
The Settings Charm   25
Shutting Down the Computer   26
Sleep Mode   27
Keyboard Shortcuts   28

3

Personalising Windows 8.1   **29**
Introduction   29
The Lock Screen   30
   Using Your Own Picture for the Lock Screen   30
Personalising the Start Screen   31
   Your Account Picture   32
   Locking the Screen   33
Changing the Desktop Background   34
Alternative Ways to Open the Control Panel   34
   Using Your Own Photos as the Desktop Background   35
Changing the Windows Border Colours   35
Changing the Size of Text and Icons, etc.   37
Changing the Screen Resolution   38

4

Ease of Access   39
The Magnifier   41
The Narrator   42
The On-Screen Keyboard   43
High Contrast   43
Opening Ease of Access from the Apps Screen   44
Speech Recognition   45
Further Help   47
Opening the Control Panel   48
    The New Start Button in Windows 8.1   48

5

Getting Connected   49
Introduction   49
Essential Equipment   50
    Internet Adaptor   50
    Internet Access Point   50
      Network Security   51
      Mobile Broadband   51
Internet Service Providers (ISPs)   52
The Web Browser   53
Making the Connection   54
    Detecting the Router or Internet Access Point 54
    Connecting to the Router   56
Troubleshooting   57
Overcoming Internet Connection Problems   58
Internet Speed   59
    Checking Your Broadband Speed   60
Connecting Printers   61

6

Using the Internet   63
Introduction   63
The Keyword Search   64
    Using the bing Search Engine   64
The New Search Feature in Windows 8.1   65
The Google Search Engine   66
Using a Web Address   67

Navigating Around a Web Site 68
    Windows 8 and RT and Windows 8.1 and RT 8.1 69
    Windows 8.1 and RT 8.1 Only 69
    The Favorites Bar — Windows 8.1 and RT 8.1 69
Tabbed Browsing 70
The Windows Store 71
    Downloading and Installing an App 73
Internet Security 75
    Windows Firewall 77
    Windows Update 77
    Windows Defender 78
    SmartScreen 78

7

Electronic Mail 79
The Windows Mail App 80
The E-mail Address 81
    Creating a New Microsoft Account 81
Receiving an E-mail 82
    The Attachment 83
Creating an E-mail 84
    Inserting an Attachment 86
Sending an E-mail 87
Responding to an E-mail 88
Using SkyDrive to Share Files 89
    Uploading Files to SkyDrive 89
    Sending a Link Via E-mail 90

8

Social Networking 91
Introduction 91
The People App 92
Introducing Facebook 93
    Facebook Friends 93
    Confidentiality and Security 93
Using Facebook from the Web Site 94

Your Facebook Profile or Timeline   96
The Audience Selector   96
Posting a Status Update   97
The Facebook App (Windows 8.1 Only)   97
Introducing Twitter   98
    What is a Tweet?   98
    Followers on Twitter   98
Using Twitter from the Web site   99
    The Twitter Icons   99
Signing Up for Twitter   100
Hashtags   101
Twitter in Use   101
Posting a Tweet   102
Reading Tweets   102
Responding to a Tweet   103
Using the Twitter App   104
    The Twitter App Home Page   104
Skype   105
    Creating a New Skype Name and Password   106

9

Software Compatibility   107
Introduction   107
The Windows Operating System   107
Upgrading Windows XP or Vista   108
    The Clean Install   108
Upgrading Windows 7   109
Upgrading Windows 8 to Windows 8.1   110
Applications Software for Windows 8.1   111
Installing Traditional Windows Software   111
Applications Software for Windows RT 8.1   113

Glossary of Terms   115

Index   117

Why Change to Windows 8.1?

Earlier versions of Windows such as Windows XP and Windows 7 are still very popular. This raises the question "why bother to change to Windows 8.1?" I have been an enthusiastic user of Windows XP and Windows 7 from their beginnings. However, I have used Windows 8.1 extensively on laptop and desktop computers (and Windows RT 8.1 on tablets) and believe they have the following advantages:

- The new Start Screen and its clearly labelled tiles are more explicit than the traditional Windows icons.

- The tiles make it easier to locate and launch programs (or *apps* in the latest jargon).

- *Live* tiles also keep you informed of the latest news and *notifications* inform you of new e-mails, etc.

- Windows 8.1 starts up faster than earlier versions of Windows. Programs also appear to run faster.

- Thousands of apps for, it seems, every conceivable purpose are available to be downloaded from the Windows Store. Many of these are free.

- Programs such as Internet Explorer, running in the Modern UI, fill the whole of the screen, with toolbars hidden in the background but viewable when required.

- Many older computers can be upgraded to run Windows 8.1 (but not to run Windows RT 8.1)

- Windows 8.1 (but not Windows RT 8.1) can run traditional Windows applications software or apps

- Windows RT 8.1 includes a special version of Office 2013, based on the world's leading office software.

It's well worth the effort to acquire the skills needed to use Windows 8.1. The Modern User Interface represents the future, being used on all types of computer from touchscreen tablets and smartphones to laptop and desktop machines.

Introducing
Windows 8.1 & RT 8.1

What is Windows?

Stored inside every computer there is a suite of software known as the *operating system*. This manages and controls every aspect of the computer's operation, no matter what *application* or *app* (such as a Web browser, music or photo editing program) you are running. The operating system provides the start up screen and various screen objects, such as icons and menu options, used to launch programs and carry out tasks such as saving and printing documents.

The operating system used in over 90% of the world's personal computers is called *Microsoft Windows*, of which there have been many versions. Usually abbreviated simply to "Windows", it is known as a *GUI (Graphical User Interface)* because it's based on small *icons* on the screen, as shown below.

In the graphical user interface, applications and documents are displayed in rectangular *windows*. These may be *maximised* to fill the whole screen or *minimised* so they appear only as icons on the Taskbar along the bottom of the screen.

The Evolution of Windows

The Windows operating system was first introduced in 1985 and subsequently evolved through several versions, including Windows 95 and Windows 98. These were followed by Windows Me in 2000 and Windows XP in 2001. Windows XP still has many users today. Windows Vista was introduced in 2007 followed in 2009 by the hugely successful Windows 7, currently used on nearly half the laptop and desktop computers in the world.

Windows 8 and RT were introduced in 2012, in response to the explosion in the use of tablet computers. Windows 8 and RT can be controlled either by *touchscreen gestures* or with the traditional mouse and keyboard. Obviously, for touchscreen operation, a touch-sensitive screen is required, as used on all tablet computers and some laptop and desktop computers. The Start Screen and Apps screens shown on the next page are known as the *Modern User Interface* or *Modern UI*, in contrast to the traditional *Desktop* used on earlier versions of Windows.

Windows 8 was designed to run on laptop and desktop PC computers as well as those tablet computers which are built to the *x64* or *x86* PC specification. Windows RT was designed for tablet computers which use the *ARM processor*. These include the Microsoft Surface, also known as the Surface RT.

Windows 8.1 and Windows RT 8.1 were launched in October 2013 and incorporate changes resulting from reviews and consumer feedback from Windows 8 and RT. These changes include the ability to start up the computer in the traditional Windows Desktop, which some people prefer. Windows 8 and RT are the same in many respects to Windows 8.1 and RT 8.1. Where there are differences, these are explained in the text.

Windows 8.1 and RT 8.1 are fast and easy to use, either by touchscreen or with a mouse and keyboard. Switching between the Modern User Interface and the traditional Windows Desktop is discussed in Chapter 2.

Windows 8.1 — The Modern UI

Shown below is the Windows 8.1 Start Screen, based on *tiles* which are tapped with a finger or clicked with a mouse, to launch programs or apps. Some tiles display live information which is regularly updated, such as news, weather and sport.

The Start Screen in Windows 8.1, shown above, has a number of default tiles, such as Internet Explorer and Skype. These tiles are automatically present as soon as Windows 8.1 is installed. In addition you can add tiles for any new apps that you install or for your favourite Web sites. Apps and Web sites are launched by a single tap with a finger or a click with the left button on a mouse.

As discussed on pages 7 and 8, all of your installed apps are displayed on the Apps screen, as shown in the extract below.

Versions of Windows 8.1

There are three versions of Windows 8.1 intended for the home user, as listed below. Another version, Windows 8.1 Enterprise, has extra features relevant to large organisations.

Windows 8.1

This is the basic or standard version, pre-installed by computer manufacturers. Individual computer builders can buy this edition on an *OEM* DVD (Original Equipment Manufacturers).

Windows 8.1 Pro

This edition has some additional features and can be used to upgrade a computer running an earlier version of Windows, such as Windows XP, Vista or Windows 7.

Windows 8.1 Pro can be downloaded and installed from the Microsoft Web site. You can also buy a retail version of Windows 8.1 Pro on a DVD and install it, as discussed in Chapter 9.

Windows 8.1 and 8.1 Pro run on computers which use the **x64** and **x86** PC processors, standard on most laptop, desktop computers and on some tablet computers.

Windows 8.1 and 8.1 Pro can run software (e.g. e-mail, Skype, spreadsheets, etc.) designed for earlier versions of Windows, such as XP, Vista and Windows 7 Pro.

Windows RT 8.1

Windows RT 8.1 is a special version of Windows 8.1, designed for the *ARM processor*, technology widely used on smartphones and tablet computers such as the Microsoft Surface.

Software has to be specially written for Windows RT 8.1. The Office 2013 suite of software has been converted to run on Windows RT 8.1 and is included with it.

Upgrading from Windows 8 to Windows 8.1

If your computer is already running Windows 8, there is a free upgrade to Windows 8.1. The upgrade is started by clicking or tapping a link in the *Windows Store*, as discussed in Chapter 9. Windows RT is upgraded to Windows RT 8.1 in the same way.

Some of the main changes introduced in Windows 8.1, relative to its predecessor, Windows 8, are as follows:

- A new Arrow button to toggle between the Start Screen and the Apps screen. (Not included in RT 8.1)

- A new Start button (discussed in Chapter 2) to toggle between the Start Screen and the current app.

- The new Start button can be right-clicked to display the shortcut menu with new options.

- An option to show the Apps screen, instead of the Start Screen, whenever the Start Screen is selected.

- An option to start the computer in Desktop mode (shown on page 8) rather than in the Start Screen.

Chapter 9 discusses the methods of upgrading a computer to Windows 8.1 from earlier versions of Windows, such as XP, Vista and Windows 7. The availability of applications software for Windows 8.1 and RT 8.1 is also discussed.

All of the versions of Windows 8.1 look the same and are operated in the same way. Therefore most of the explanations in this book apply to all of the versions of Windows 8.1 listed on page 4 (and also to their predecessors in the Windows 8 family). Where there are differences between the versions of Windows, separate notes are included.

In the remainder of this book, except where otherwise stated, the term Windows 8.1 will include all versions listed on page 4.

The Microsoft Surface and Surface Pro

When Windows 8 was launched in 2012, Microsoft also announced two new tablet computers, the Surface and the Surface Pro. As discussed shortly, the Surface and the Surface Pro have different technical specifications. However, the two systems look the same and are operated in the same way.

The Surface and Surface Pro are operated by touchscreen gestures and an *on-screen keyboard*. Both Surface tablets also have a special cover which can double up as a separate keyboard and touchpad. In addition, the Surface and Surface Pro each have a *USB port*, allowing a range of external devices to be connected, such as a keyboard, mouse, printer and flash drive.

The basic Surface tablet uses a special version of Windows 8.1, known as Windows RT 8.1 and discussed earlier. The Surface Pro uses the same technology as traditional laptop and desktop PC computers and runs Windows 8.1 Pro. Unlike the basic Surface (RT 8.1) tablet, the Surface Pro can use applications software or apps designed for earlier versions of Windows, such as Windows XP, Vista and Windows 7, as discussed earlier.

Viewing All of Your Apps

Windows 8 and RT

All of the apps installed on your computer can be displayed using the **All apps** icon shown on the right. To display the icon on a touchscreen, from the Start Screen shown on page 3, swipe in from the top or bottom edge. Alternatively, with a mouse, right-

click over the Start Screen to display the **All apps** icon. Then tap or click the icon to reveal all of the apps. Flick the screen with a finger or drag the horizontal scroll bar at the bottom of the screen, if necessary, to view another part of the **Apps** screen.

Windows 8.1 — the Arrow Button

On this version of Windows, a new Arrow button has been added, as shown on the right. This appears below the lower left of the Start Screen on the Modern User Interface, as shown below.

Clicking the new Arrow button shown on the previous page opens the Apps screen shown on page 7. The Arrow button appears at the lower left of the Apps screen, but with the arrow now pointing upwards. Clicking this button again returns you to the Start Screen shown at the top of page 3.

Windows RT 8.1

Swipe up from the middle of the Start Screen to open the Apps screen. Swipe down from the middle of the Apps to return to the Start Screen.

The Traditional Windows Desktop

Windows XP, Vista and Windows 7, etc., have a user interface known as the *Windows Desktop*, shown below, designed to be used with a mouse and keyboard. Programs are launched by clicking on a pop-up Start menu on the left-hand side of the screen or by double-clicking icons (as shown on the right) on the main Desktop screen.

Programs currently running or frequently used appear on the *Taskbar* along the bottom of the Desktop, as shown below.

Using the Desktop in Windows 8.1

Although Windows 8.1 boots up by default in the new Start Screen shown on page 3, the traditional Desktop, shown at the bottom of page 8, is still present. It can be displayed by tapping or clicking the Desktop tile on the Start Screen, shown on the left in the extract below.

Starting Windows 8.1 in the Desktop

Right-click or tap and hold a blank area of the Taskbar at the bottom of the Desktop. From the pop-up menus, select **Properties** and **Navigation**. Then make sure the line ending "**go to the desktop instead of Start**" is ticked. The computer will now start up displaying the Desktop rather than the Start Screen.

Start screen

☑ When I sign in or close all applications on a screen, go to the desktop instead of Start

☐ Show my desktop background on Start

☐ Show Start on the display I'm using when I press the Windows logo key

☐ Show the Apps view automatically when I go to Start

Go to the Apps Screen Instead of the Start Screen

As shown above, at the bottom, there is also an option to default straight to the Apps screen (shown on page 7 and 8) instead of the Start Screen, whenever the Start Screen is selected.

Tiles on the Start Screen

This is the most striking change between Windows 8.1 and earlier versions such as Windows XP and Windows 7. On starting up, by default the familiar Desktop is replaced by the new Start Screen of the Modern User Interface. Gone are the previous Start Menu and Taskbar, to be replaced by a matrix of square and rectangular tiles, shown in the sample below.

The tile shown on the right is used to open the Microsoft Web browser, Internet Explorer 11. The program is launched by tapping the tile with a finger or clicking with a mouse. Internet Explorer 11 is included with Windows 8.1 and the tile shown on the right appears on the Start Screen by default.

When you install additional apps from the Windows Store, tiles for them are automatically created on the Start Screen. As discussed later, you can also *pin* tiles for apps and Web sites to the Start Screen. Then apps or Web sites can be opened quickly by a single tap with a finger or a click of the left mouse button.

Live Tiles

Some tiles, such as **News**, **Sport**, **Weather** and **Finance** display constantly changing headlines and live information. A sample headline on the **Finance** tile is shown on the right. After a few seconds the headlines in the **Finance** tile change, to display the FTSE index, as shown below right. Tapping or clicking the **Finance** tile leads to a full screen of news reports, as shown in the example below. To scroll through the news items, swipe across the screen or use a mouse to drag the horizontal scroll bar, as shown at the bottom of the screen shot below.

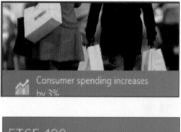

Spain does not need a bailout - Luis de Guindos	Focus on Germany as EADS, BAE inch closer to deal	Business spooked by UK tax avoidance clampdown	BP/	BP PLC
BBC NEWS 12 HOURS AGO	REUTERS UK 11 HOURS AGO	THE GUARDIAN 22 HOURS AGO	▲436.98	+2.78 +0.64%
Spain's economy minister Luis de Guindos has denied that his country needs a bailout. His speech in London was interrupted by a group of protesters who waved placards...	BERLIN/PARIS, Oct 5 (Reuters) - EADS and BAE Systems have edged closer towards winning...	LONDON (Reuters) - The activists who have protested in recent months at the tax arrangements...	BARC	Barclays PLC
			▲223.94	+1.39 +0.62%
Profits fall? In 20yrs we'll be world's No1	World food prices rise, stay close to crisis levels-FAO	American Airlines, pilots resume labour talks amid turmoil	VOD	Vodafone Group PLC
THE SUN 8 HOURS AGO	THE GUARDIAN 23 HOURS AGO	REUTERS UK 1 DAY AGO	▲180.40	+2.40 +1.35%
TESCO has vowed to bounce back from its first profits fall for nearly 20 years — by becoming the biggest retailer in the WORLD. Boss Phil Clarke told Sun City yesterday...	ROME (Reuters) - World food prices rose in September and are seen remaining close to levels reached during the 2008 food crisis, the United Nations' food agency said...	(Reuters) - American Airlines and its pilots union resumed contract talks Wednesday, but other problems...	LLOY	Lloyds Banking Group...
Last Updated @ 05 October 2012 10:17:41 Quotes delayed			▼37.86	-0.16 -0.43%

As discussed in Chapter 2, there are several ways to return to the Start Screen at any time or to launch new apps. You can have several apps running in the background at the same time and cycle through them, before switching to a different app on the screen. You can easily close running apps but this is not essential as they are closed when the computer is shut down.

The Travel App

When you tap or click the **Travel** tile, you can choose from an array of small images of the world's major cities. The **Destinations** feature shows full screen photos such as **Venice** below and you

can also see 360 degree panoramic views of major attractions.

The **Travel** app also lists hotels, restaurants and tourist information, as shown below.

The Mail App

Many of the apps which appear as tiles on the Start Screen are discussed in more detail later in this book. The **Mail** tile leads to a new, fully featured e-mail program as

shown below. E-mail is discussed in more detail in Chapter 7.

The People App

This helps you to keep in touch with friends on social networking sites such as Facebook and Twitter. Social networking is discussed in detail in Chapter 8.

The Weather App

This allows you to find out 10-day weather forecasts for any selected location, both where you live or worldwide.

The SkyDrive App

SkyDrive is a storage facility on the Internet where you can place copies of your documents and photos, etc. This means they can be shared with friends, family or colleagues anywhere in the world. All they need is an Internet connection and a Web browser on any device such as a smartphone, tablet computer, laptop or  desktop machine. This remote storage of documents, etc., is known as *cloud computing* and discussed in Chapter 7.

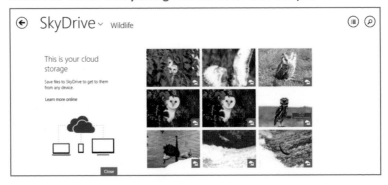

Many more apps are included with Windows 8.1 itself, while others can be downloaded from the *Windows Store* as discussed in Chapter 6.

Some Utility Apps in Windows 8.1

The *Windows Explorer* used in previous versions of Windows is still present in Windows 8.1, though it is now known as the *File Explorer*. This is used to manage all of your documents and other files in a hierarchical system of folders.

Also present in Windows 8.1 are the graphics programs *Windows Paint* and *Fresh Paint* and the *Control Panel*, discussed later in this book, used to manage the computer and the settings for various devices.

Navigating Windows 8.1

Introduction

You can use all editions of Windows 8.1 (including Windows RT 8.1) with a touchscreen or with a mouse and keyboard. Users of tablet computers may be able to choose between these two modes of operation, while many desktop and laptop computers can only be controlled by a mouse and keyboard. To use touch operation with a laptop or desktop computer, a special touch-sensitive screen is required.

When you switch the computer on, it quickly boots, i.e. starts up, to display the Lock Screen, shown below. (Alternative Lock Screen designs can be selected, as discussed in Chapter 3). Either swipe your finger diagonally across a touchscreen or click anywhere on the screen if using a mouse. Then enter the password for your Microsoft account. This is set up during the sign-up process when Windows 8.1 is first installed.

The next two pages list some common Windows 8.1 mouse operations and the corresponding touchscreen *gestures*.

Basic Mouse Operations

Click

Press the left mouse button to select an object on the screen at the current cursor position, such as a menu option. Opens an app from its tile on the Start Screen.

Double-click

Two left clicks in quick succession to open a folder in the Windows (or File) Explorer. Also launches an app from an icon.

Right-click

Press the right mouse button to open a shortcut or context sensitive menu. These menus list options relevant to the current cursor position.

Drag

Click over a screen object, then keeping the left button held down drag the object to a new position, before releasing the left button. Can be used to change the position of a tile on the Start Screen or move a file or folder to a different folder in the File Explorer (also known as the Windows Explorer). Drag is also used to move horizontal or vertical scroll bars to advance forwards or backwards through a long document. Dragging an object to another disc drive, *copies* the object. Dragging an object to a new location on the same disc drive *moves* the object. Dragging with the right button held down displays a menu when the button is released. This includes options to move or copy the item.

Scroll Wheel

This wheel in the centre of a mouse is used to scroll through a long document on the screen.

Ctrl + Scroll Wheel

Hold down the Ctrl key and turn the scroll wheel. This zooms in or out of whatever is currently displayed on the screen.

Basic Touch Gestures

Tap

Press quickly but gently on the screen to launch an app from a tile on the Start Screen, or select an option from a menu.

Double Tap

Two quick taps to open a folder or flash drive, etc., in Windows File Explorer. To find out about devices such as a printer, double tap its icon in Devices and Printers in the Control Panel.

Tap and Hold

Keep your finger gently pressing against an object or area of the screen for a few seconds then release to display a shortcut menu relevant to the current screen location.

Drag

Keeping your finger over a screen object such as a tile on the Start Screen or a file in the File Explorer, move your finger over the screen and release to drop the object in its new location.

Swipe

This involves sliding your finger across the screen, usually from one of the four edges. Swiping has many uses for displaying running apps and options and these are discussed in detail shortly.

Flick

The finger is quickly moved across the screen horizontally or vertically to scroll through a long document.

Rotate two fingers to turn an object.

Pinch or move two fingers together to zoom out.

Stretch or move two fingers apart to zoom in or enlarge.

The *bezel* or border around a tablet screen is touch sensitive. When you swipe from the left, right, top or bottom edge of the screen, always start with your finger in the bezel area.

Launching Apps Using Tiles

After you enter your password, the Start Screen appears as shown below. The background colour can be changed if you wish, as discussed in Chapter 3.

If you want to change the position of a particular tile, it can be dragged and dropped to a new position, as mentioned on the previous pages.

To launch a particular app, such as Internet Explorer shown below, tap or click its tile, as shown on the right.

Returning to the Start Screen from an App

The New Start Button in Windows 8.1

Some users of Windows 8 said they missed the Start button, used to launch programs in Windows 7, etc. Windows 8.1 introduced a new Start button, on the bottom left-hand corner of the screen. As shown on the right, the Start button uses the Windows logo and appears on the left of the Taskbar at the bottom of the Desktop, as shown below.

In Windows 8.1 and 8.1 Pro the Start button also appears as shown on the right, when you let the cursor hover over the bottom left-hand corner of the Start Screen. Clicking the Start button switches backwards and forwards between the current app and the Start Screen.

The Start button doesn't appear on the Start Screen in Windows RT 8.1. However, there are several other methods of switching between the current app and the Start Screen.

- On the Surface and Surface Pro use the Windows logo button on the bezel at the bottom of the screen.

- Use the Windows logo key on a keyboard.

- Use the Start *Charm*, shown on the right, on the Charms Bar, as discussed on page 23.

The Start Menu in Windows 8.1

Right-click the new Start button, shown at the top of this page, to display a large menu, including the option to **Shut down**. The **Control Panel** is used for many important computer settings and the **File Explorer** is used to

Task Manager	
Control Panel	
File Explorer	Sign out
Search	Sleep
Run	Shut down
Shut down or sign out ▸	Restart
Desktop	

manage your documents, photos and other files.

Launching an App

Typing the First Few Letters of the App's Name

If you're using a separate physical keyboard, with the Start Screen displayed, start typing the App's name. For example, to launch the Notepad app, as soon as you've typed **note**, a link to open the app is immediately displayed.

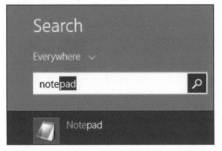

With a touchscreen, tap the Search Charm, as shown on the right, after swiping in from the right-hand bezel. Then use the on-screen keyboard to start typing the first few letters of the app, until a link

appears as shown above with a purple background. Tap or click inside the **Notepad** link shown above to launch the app.

Using an Icon on the Apps Screen

Display the Apps screen as discussed on page 7. Then tap or click the required icon to launch the app.

Pinning a Tile for an App to the Start Screen

With a mouse, right-click the icon for the app in the Apps screen. With the touchscreen in Windows RT 8.1, tap and hold the icon for the app.

From the toolbar which appears along the bottom of the screen, tap or click **Pin to Start**, as shown on the right. The app can now be launched by clicking or tapping the tile on the Start Screen.

Switching Apps

You can have lots of apps running in the background at the same time. To cycle through the apps that are currently running, swipe in from the left-hand edge, starting from the bezel. With a mouse, keep clicking in the top left-hand corner. The apps are displayed one at a time on the full screen. Stop at the app you want to use.

Swipe in a few centimetres from the left-hand edge and back again to see thumbnails of all the apps currently running, as shown down the left-hand edge below. Or hover the cursor over the top or bottom left corner then move the cursor up or down the left edge of the screen. Alternatively hold down the Windows Logo key and press the Tab key. Tap or click on a thumbnail as shown down the left-hand side below to switch to the new app.

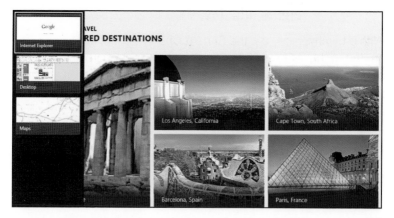

Holding down Alt and pressing Tab displays all the running apps as thumbnails across the centre of the screen, as shown below. Stop pressing Tab and release the Alt key when you have highlighted the app you want to run on the full screen.

Displaying Two or More Apps Side by Side

In Windows 8.1 you can have up to 4 apps running side by side in separate windows. This *multi-tasking* is useful, for example, while making notes with a word processor in one window using data extracted from a spreadsheet running in the other window.

From the Start Screen, open an app on the full screen. Drag or swipe the top of the app downwards and to the left or the right. The app then appears in a window filling half the screen, with a vertical line separating the apps.

Open the Start Screen again and open a second app. This fills the other half of the screen. If you wish to alter the size of each window, drag the black vertical bar in the centre of the screen. The windows can be divided in the ratios 50/50, 60/40 and 70/30.

You can open a third app which can be dragged and dropped to replace one of the first two apps. If you want to open all three apps at the same time, drag or swipe the third app until a space opens up for the third app. If a space doesn't open up, your screen can only support two apps open at the same time.

Depending on the resolution of your screen, you can have 2, 3 or 4 apps running in separate windows side by side on the screen.

The Charms Bar

Swipe in from the right-hand edge of the screen to reveal the Charms Bar shown on the right. Alternatively use a mouse to hover the cursor in either the bottom right or top right corner of the screen. Then move the cursor upwards or downwards through the charms to display the charms against a black background, as shown on the right. The physical keyboard on the Surface tablet has keys for each of the charms. Alternatively, if you have a suitable keyboard, hold down the Windows Logo key and press **C** to display the Charms Bar.

The Search Charm

Tap or click the **Search** charm shown on the top right above to begin looking for information. The original search feature in Windows 8 and Windows RT has been modified in Windows 8.1 and Windows RT 8.1 as discussed below and on the next page.

Searching in Windows 8 and RT

As shown on the right, when you select the **Search** charm in Windows 8 or RT, a list of categories of information stored on your computer or on the Internet is displayed. Searching within **Apps**, shown on the right near the top, was also discussed on page 20. There are also several other categories to search through, such as **Settings**, **Files**, **Finance** and **Internet Explorer** as shown on the right. Tap or click the required category, such as **Internet Explorer**, then enter the keyword for the search.

In the example on the right, with **News** selected, the keywords **Gas prices** were entered into the Search bar. When you tap or click the magnifying glass search icon, a large selection of the latest

headlines and extracts from newspapers is displayed, as shown below. Drag or swipe to see all of the headlines and abstracts.

Searching in Windows 8.1 and RT 8.1

Open the search bar from the Search charm as before, or with the Start Screen displayed, *type a keyword* to search for, such as **Entrevaux**, for example. By default, the search looks Everywhere for results. To search within a category tap or click **Everywhere** and from the drop-down menu select the category, e.g. **Settings** or **Files**, as shown on the right below. The results of a search in Windows 8.1 and RT 8.1 show more information than those in Windows 8 and RT, as discussed on page 65.

The **Share** option on the Charms Bar on page 23 allows you to share information or photos, etc., with other people, using e-mail or social networking.

Start on the Charms Bar returns you to the Start Screen. If you're already on the Start Screen, the computer switches to the most recent app.

Devices on the Charms Bar lists any printers, speakers, etc., connected to the computer or on a home network. These only appear when you are using an app with something to print, such as the **Mail** app.

The Settings Charm

The **Settings** charm shown below on the right and on the Charms Bar on page 23 leads to some of the most important settings on your computer.

When you select the **Settings** charm shown on the right, the icons shown below appear at the bottom right of the screen. These give information about your Internet connection, (e.g. **BTHomeHub...**) and your sound and brightness settings, for example.

Change PC settings shown on the bottom right below leads to a list called **PC settings** as shown on the next page.

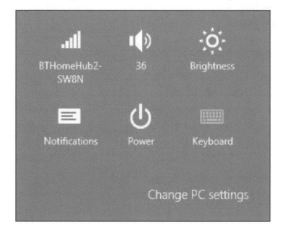

Personalise shown below provides different colour schemes and designs for your screens. **Ease of Access** near the bottom of the screen shot below allows you to make adjustments and select features designed to help with special needs.

The Windows 8.1 PC settings window shown above is slightly different from the Windows 8 version.

Shutting Down the Computer

At the end of a computing session always shut down correctly. Otherwise you might damage any files that are open. Select the **Settings** charm as discussed on the previous page and tap or click the **Power** icon shown on the right above and in context below. Then tap or click **Shut down** from the small menu which pops up, as shown on the right. (**Update and shut down** is displayed if an update is available). This closes all apps that are currently running and switches off the computer.

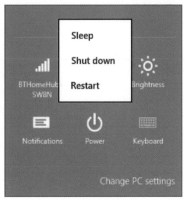

Sleep Mode

Selecting **Sleep** on the small **Power** menu at the bottom of the previous page puts the computer in a low power consumption mode. This saves electricity while you are not using the computer. Your work and settings are saved and to resume work later press the power button on your computer.

Your computer will enter Sleep mode automatically if it is not used for a period of time. This is set in the Control Panel which can be opened from the menu shown at the bottom of page 19. Then select **Hardware and Sound/Power Options/Edit Plan Settings** to display the following window.

Change settings for the plan: Balanced

Choose the sleep and display settings that you want your computer to use.

	On battery	Plugged in
☉ Dim the display:	1 minute ⌄	1 minute ⌄
☽ Put the computer to sleep:	2 minutes ⌄	2 minutes ⌄
☼ Adjust plan brightness:	○ ○ ☼	○ ○ ☼

Tap or click the arrow on the right of **2 minutes** shown above to display a menu of optional time periods, ranging from 1 minute to 5 hours before Sleep mode is launched. There is also a **Never** option. Select the required time and tap or click **Save changes**.

Sleep mode is useful if you want to leave your computer for a while and the screen is displaying confidential information. When you return, press the power button and the computer will resume where you left off with the same files, documents and apps running. The Control Panel can be used to set the Lock Screen (shown on page 15) to appear when the power button is pressed. Swipe diagonally across or click anywhere on the Lock Screen, then enter your password to resume your previous activities.

Keyboard Shortcuts

If you use a keyboard like the one below with keys such as **Ctrl**, **Alt**, **Tab** and the Windows Logo key, shown on the right, you may find the following key presses useful as alternatives to the touchscreen or mouse, etc.

Keyboard Shortcuts

Alt+F4   Close the current app.

Alt+Tab   Cycle through all open Desktop and Modern UI apps displayed horizontally across the screen.

F1   Help.

Win   Alternate between current app and the Start Screen.

Win+C   Display the Charms Bar.

Win+F   Search files.

Win+X   Display shortcuts menu.

Win+Tab   Display the apps which are currently running, as thumbnails down the left of the screen.

Example:

Alt+F4 means: "While holding down the **Alt** key, press the **F4** key".

Personalising Windows 8.1

Introduction

Windows 8.1 provides a number of ways for you to customise your computer to suit your own particular needs and preferences, such as:

- Selecting a different background design for the Lock Screen. The Lock Screen appears when you first start the computer or if you wake it up from sleep mode.

- Changing the colour scheme for the Start Screen. This is the main screen used to launch apps, shown on page 18.

- Creating or changing your account picture used to identify you, e.g. by including it in the e-mails you send.

- Selecting a different background design for the Windows Desktop, which was discussed on pages 8 and 9.

- Changing the colour scheme for the windows borders and the Taskbar along the bottom of the Desktop.

- Changing the *screen resolution*. This is the number of *pixels* or picture elements in the horizontal and vertical directions. Windows 8.1 requires a minimum resolution of 1024x768 pixels, with more needed for some tasks.

- Using the Ease of Access Center, which provides features to help anyone with special needs, such as the magnifier to enlarge text and the on-screen keyboard for anyone struggling to use a physical keyboard.

The Lock Screen

This is the screen which appears when the computer starts up or when you wake it from sleep. Open the Charms bar as described on page 23 and from the Settings charm, shown on the right, select **Change PC settings**. Then select the **Lock screen** panel, as shown below. With **Lock screen** preview displayed at the top of the screen you can see the current design in the main panel, while along the bottom there's a choice of different Lock Screens.

Using Your Own Picture for the Lock Screen

If you don't wish to use any of the designs provided, select **Browse** to search the images on your computer, etc. Then select with a tick the picture you wish to use and tap or click **Choose picture**, as shown below.

Personalising the Start Screen

Windows 8 & RT

In Windows 8 you can change the colour scheme for the Start Screen. Select **Start Screen** from the top right of the screen, as shown below then experiment with different colours on the horizontal bar at the bottom..

PC settings

Lock screen   Start screen   Account picture

Personalise

Users

Notifications

Search

Share

General

Privacy

Devices

Wireless

Ease of Access

Windows 8.1 & RT 8.1

With the Start Screen displayed tap or click the **Settings** charm as discussed on the previous page. Then select **Personalise** from the top of the right-hand panel. Various colour schemes appear in the right-hand panel with sliders allowing you to change the background colours and designs, as shown below.

In Windows 8.1 there is an option, **Show my desktop background on Start**, as shown at the bottom of page 9.

Your Account Picture

You can create or change your account picture in Windows 8 & RT after selecting **Account picture**, as shown below on the top right.

PC settings

Lock screen   Start screen   Account picture

Personalise

Users

Notifications

Search

Share

Browse

General

Create an account picture

Privacy

Camera

Devices

In Windows 8.1 and RT 8.1 select the **Settings** charm, then **Change PC settings**, then tap or click **Account picture**.

If you've a suitable image stored on your computer's hard disc or on a removable disc or flash drive, select **Browse**, as shown above under the picture, to search for and insert the image. Select with a tick the image you wish to use then select **Choose image**.

Alternatively if you have a tablet or laptop computer with a built-in camera or a desktop machine with a plug-in webcam, tap or click the camera icon shown on the right and above to create a new account photo.

Your account picture appears in several places, such as the Welcome screen as the computer starts up, on the right-hand side of the Start Screen, as shown on the right and on the top of any e-mails you send using the Windows Mail app.

Locking the Screen

If you tap or click your account picture on the Start Screen, a small menu pops up as shown below.

Change account picture shown above opens the PC settings window shown on the previous page. **Account picture** is already selected and the picture can be changed after selecting **Browse** as described on the previous page.

If you select **Lock** shown above, the Lock Screen is displayed. The computer can now only be used by someone who knows the password. This is entered after swiping upwards from the bottom of a touchscreen or with a mouse, clicking anywhere on the screen.

Sign out shown in the top screenshot also returns you to the Lock Screen shown on the right above and requires a new user to sign in, as shown on the right.

Changing the Desktop Background

Tap or click the **Desktop** tile on the **Start Screen**, then select the **Settings** charm and tap or click **Control Panel** at the top of the right-hand panel. Under **Appearance and Personalisation**, select **Change desktop background**. Windows provides several designs for the Desktop background. If you select more than one, the background takes the form of a slide show.

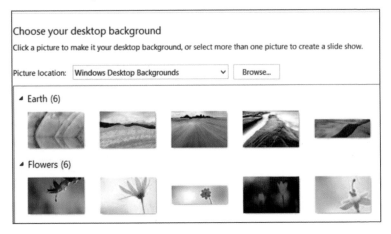

Alternatively, Tap or click the Desktop tile and select the **Settings** charm and this time tap or click **Personalisation** at the top of the right-hand panel.

This provides several **Themes** allowing you to change the background colour, sounds and screensaver all at once.

Alternative Ways to Open the Control Panel

Right-click or tap and hold in the extreme bottom left-hand corner of the screen and then select **Control Panel** from the shortcut menu, as shown on page 48. Alternatively right-click or tap and hold over **Control Panel** in the **Apps** screen as discussed earlier and select **Pin to Start**. This places a tile on the Start Screen for opening the **Control Panel**.

Using Your Own Photos as the Desktop Background

Select the **Browse** button as shown in the screenshot on the previous page, then locate the folder containing the photo(s) you want to

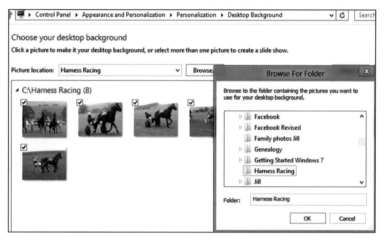

use. In the example below, after selecting the hard disc **(C:)**, the folder **Harness Racing** was opened by tapping (or clicking) **OK**.

All of the required photos were selected with a tick in the top left-hand corner as shown above, so the Desktop background will be a slide show. For a constant background, only tick one photo. Select **Save changes** to complete setting the new background.

Changing the Windows Border Colours

This includes the colour of the Taskbar along the bottom of the Windows Desktop. Open the Control Panel as described on the previous page. Select the green heading **Appearance and Personalization** and then under **Personalisation** select **Change the colour of your taskbar and window borders**.

Personalisation
Change the theme   Change desktop background
Change the colour of your taskbar and window borders   Change sound effects

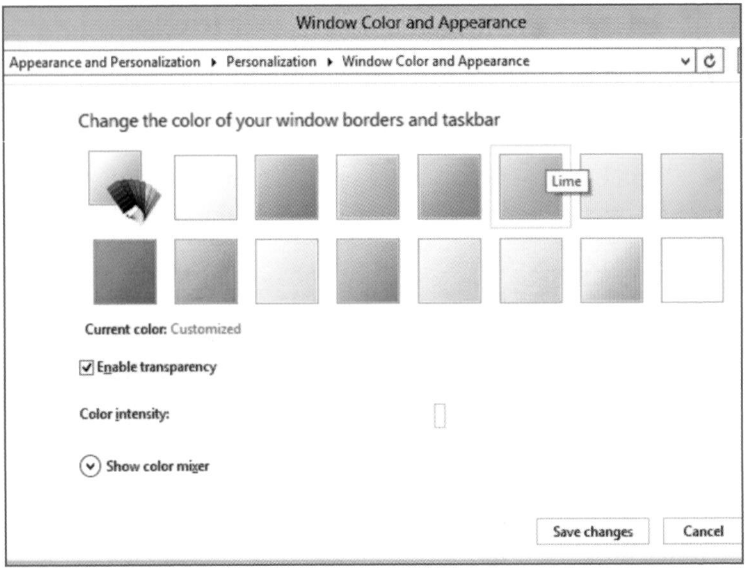

Before finally selecting a colour for your windows' borders and the Taskbar along the bottom of the Desktop, you may wish to experiment with **transparency**, **Color intensity** and the **color mixer**, as shown above. Then select **Save changes** to put the new settings into effect. In the example below, the colour **Twilight** was chosen for the border and the Taskbar, with transparency disabled and the intensity set at high.

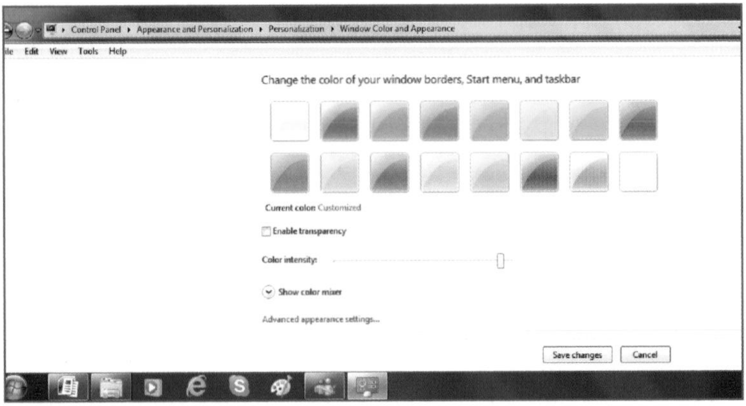

Changing the Size of Text and Icons, etc.

If you're finding the text and other items difficult to see on the screen, there are ways of enlarging them. From the **Control Panel** select **Appearance and Personalisation**, followed by **Display** and then **Make text and other items larger or smaller**.

 Display
Make text and other items larger or smaller   Adjust screen resolution

The **Display** window opens, as shown below. To change the size of all of the objects on the screen including icons, images and text, select **Custom sizing options**. Then either select a different percentage or drag the ruler which appears. To change only the size of the text in windows, for example in the title bars or in menu options, use the drop-down menu under **Change the text size only**. As discussed shortly, the **Magnifier** allows you to enlarge a small selected area of the screen.

Change the size of all items

You can make text and other items on the desktop bigger by choosing one of these options. To temporarily enlarge just part of the screen, use the Magnifier tool.

○ Smaller - 100% (default)

◉ Medium - 125%

Custom sizing options

Change the text size only

Instead of changing the size of everything on the desktop, change only the text size for a specific item.

| Title bars ∨ | 11 ∨ | ☐ Bold |

Title bars
Menus
Message boxes   not fit on the screen.   Apply
Palette titles
Icons
Tooltips

The text on a tablet or touchscreen may be enlarged or made smaller using two-fingered stretching or pinching gestures.

Changing the Screen Resolution

A *pixel* (picture element) is a single point in a screen display. The screen resolution is usually quoted in the format 1024x768, representing the number of pixels in the horizontal and vertical directions respectively. 1024x768 is stated as the minimum resolution for Windows 8.1 with 1366x768 recommended for some applications. At the higher resolutions, objects appear sharper and smaller. The maximum resolution available depends on the specification of the monitor and the graphics components in the computer which control the screen display.

To check the resolution on your computer, from the **Appearance and Personalization** section in the **Control Panel**, as discussed earlier, select **Display** and **Adjust screen resolution**, as shown at the top of the previous page. To change the setting, tap or click the small arrow to the right of the current **Resolution** setting and drag the slider. Then select **Apply** at the bottom right of the Screen Resolution window and either **Keep changes** or **Revert**.

Ease of Access

This chapter describes features in Windows which are designed to help people with special needs, such as impaired eyesight, defective hearing or reduced manual dexterity.

The Magnifier

This makes the screen easier to read by enlarging the entire screen area or just selected parts.

The On-Screen Keyboard

This is intended for anyone who finds the normal physical keyboard difficult to use.

The Narrator

This reads aloud the text on the screen including the title bars and text in Windows as well as documents you're working on.

High Contrast

Text and backgrounds can be displayed in a choice of themes which use different colours, as shown on page 44.

Speech Recognition

You control the computer and input data entirely by speaking.

These features are discussed in more detail shortly. You can launch some of the features quickly after selecting the **Settings** charm, then **Change PC settings** and **Ease of Access** as shown on pages 25 and 44. More settings for the Ease of Access features are found in the Control Panel. Open the Control Panel as described on page 48. At the bottom right of the Control Panel there are links to the **Ease of Access** features, as shown on the right.

Ease of Access
Let Windows suggest settings
Optimise visual display

If you select **Let Windows suggest settings**, shown at the bottom of the previous page, you are presented with a series of statements about any limitations you might have, such as defective eyesight, hearing or manual dexterity.

> **Eyesight (1 of 5)**
>
> Select all statements that apply to you:
>
> ☑ Images and text on TV are difficult to see (even when I'm wearing glasses).
>
> ☐ Lighting conditions make it difficult to see images on my monitor.
>
> ☐ I am blind.
>
> ☐ I have another type of vision impairment (even if glasses correct it).

After completing the on-screen statements, Windows recommends a series of settings based on the ticks you have placed in the check boxes, covering the whole range of common impairments. You can accept or reject these settings.

Alternatively select **Ease of Access** as shown at the bottom of page 39, then select **Ease of Access Center**, as shown below.

> Ease of Access Center
> Let Windows suggest settings   Optimise visual display   Replace sounds with visual cues
> Change how your mouse works   Change how your keyboard works

The **Ease of Access Center** is used to start the **Magnifier**, **On-Screen Keyboard**, **Narrator** and **High Contrast** screen.

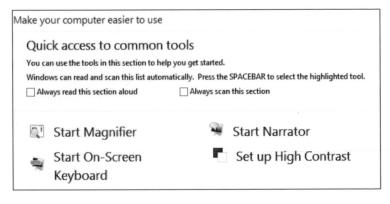

Make your computer easier to use

Quick access to common tools

You can use the tools in this section to help you get started.

Windows can read and scan this list automatically. Press the SPACEBAR to select the highlighted tool.

☐ Always read this section aloud   ☐ Always scan this section

Start Magnifier   Start Narrator

Start On-Screen   Set up High Contrast
Keyboard

The Magnifier

Tap or click **Start Magnifier**, as shown on the previous page. The **Magnifier** window opens, initially set at 100% but this can easily be changed using the plus and minus buttons shown below.

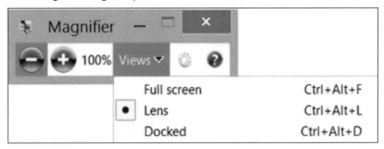

If you tap or click the arrow next to **Views**, shown above, you can choose whether to enlarge the **Full screen** or just the **Lens**. The Lens is a small rectangle which can be dragged around the screen with a finger or mouse, enlarging different areas. The example below uses 200% magnification.

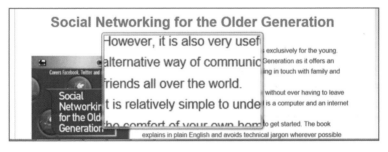

In **Docked** mode a horizontal strip across the top the screen is enlarged. This can be scrolled to display the whole document in large text. After a short time the Magnifier window shown at the top of this page changes to a magnifying glass icon, as shown on the right. This icon can be tapped or clicked to make the Magnifier window reappear on the screen. Tap or click the cross at the top right of the Magnifier window to switch off the Magnifier.

The Narrator

Tap or click **Start Narrator**, as shown at the bottom of page 40. The computer starts to read aloud all of the text on the screen. You also hear the name of any key you press. The Narrator appears as an icon on the Taskbar on the Desktop as shown on the right and below.

If you tap or click the Narrator icon, the **Narrator Settings** window opens, as shown below. This includes options to alter the speed, pitch and volume of the Narrator voice or to choose a different voice altogether. The Narrator is closed by tapping or clicking the cross in the top right-hand corner of the Narrator Settings window. Alternatively tap or click **Exit** at the bottom of the window.

Narrator Settings	— ☐ X

❓

Welcome to Narrator

Press any key on the keyboard to hear the name of that key. Press Caps Lock + F1 to review the full set of Narrator commands. Press the Tab key to navigate through the options. Press Caps Lock + Esc to exit Narrator.

General
Change how Narrator starts and other standard settings

Navigation
Change how you interact with your PC using Narrator

Voice
Change the speed, pitch or volume of the current voice or choose a new voice

Commands
Create your own keyboard commands

Minimize
Minimize this window and return to your app

Exit
Exit Narrator

The On-Screen Keyboard

If you have trouble using a physical keyboard, the **On-Screen Keyboard**, shown below in Microsoft Word, can be operated with a mouse, joystick or another pointing device.

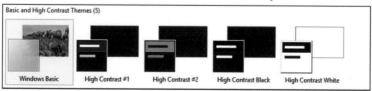

Upper and lower case letters and alternate characters on a key can be obtained by first tapping or clicking either **Caps** or **Shift**. If you have a touchscreen computer such as the Microsoft Surface, you may find it easier to use the larger keys on the virtual keyboard provided as standard with the computer.

High Contrast

Select **Set up High Contrast** as shown on page 40 and then **Choose a High Contrast Theme**. Experiment by selecting and applying different Themes to find one that suits you.

As mentioned earlier, you can quickly open the Ease of Access settings from the **Settings** charm, as discussed on pages 25 and 26. After selecting **Change PC settings**, select **Ease of Access** under **PC settings**. Then select **High Contrast** and tap or click the arrow under **Choose a theme** and select a colour scheme such as **High Contrast #2** shown below.

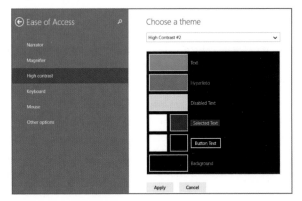

After tapping or clicking **Apply**, everything on your screen will be displayed in the colours of your chosen theme.

Opening Ease of Access from the Apps Screen

The Ease of Access features are listed on the Apps screen. Open the Apps screen, as discussed on page 7. Then scroll across the **Apps** screen until you see the **Windows Ease of Access** features such as the **Magnifier**, etc., as shown on the right. Tap or click to launch the **Magnifier**, **Narrator** or **On-Screen Keyboard**, as discussed earlier. **Windows Speech Recognition** is discussed on the next page.

Speech Recognition

This feature allows you to control the computer entirely by spoken commands. The necessary sound facilities are normally built into a tablet or laptop computer but on a desktop machine you may need to add speakers and a microphone. Tasks such as starting programs and opening menus, dictating text and writing and sending e-mails can be achieved without using a touchpad, mouse or keyboard. First you need to learn some spoken commands, by following the Windows Speech Tutorial; you must also "train" the computer to recognise your voice and dialect if you have one.

Tap or click **Speech Recognition** from Ease of Access in the Control Panel, as discussed earlier, as shown below.

The main **Speech Recognition** window is shown below.

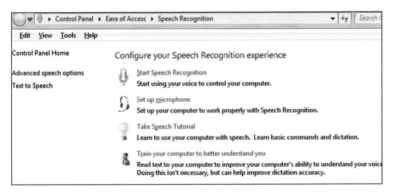

Experienced users can click **Start Speech Recognition** or beginners can select **Take Speech Tutorial** as shown above. You can also launch this feature by tapping or clicking **Windows Speech Recognition** on the Apps screen discussed on page 44.

As shown on the previous page, there is a **Set up microphone** option. When you first start Speech Recognition you are given advice on the use of the microphone and you are asked to read a piece of sample text. The Speech Tutorial helps you to practise all of the basic spoken commands such as **Start Listening**, **New Line**, **New Paragraph** and **Correct**. You are given practice at correcting mistakes on the screen and shown how to use voice commands to select menus. Selecting **Train your computer to better understand you** shown on the previous page, launches extensive practice exercises in which you speak into the microphone, while the computer learns to recognise your voice.

After you've finished training yourself (and the computer) you are ready to tap or click **Start Speech Recognition** as shown on the previous page; this displays the microphone user window shown below:

The user gives voice commands such as **Start listening** to make the computer begin interpreting the commands spoken into the microphone. The microphone button shown on the left above changes colour – blue indicating that the computer is listening to you, grey indicating not listening. The small window in the centre gives text feedback such as **Listening** or **Sleeping**. The message **What was that?** shown in the text window below indicates that a command was not understood by the computer.

If the above message appears you are advised to repeat the command or try a different command.

The Speech Recognition feature allows anyone who can't manipulate a mouse, touchpad or keyboard to use programs such as Microsoft Word, or e-mail, for example. Using only spoken commands, you can create, edit, save and print documents. I have found it quite easy to use the Speech Recognition system to dictate fairly simple documents. Although a microphone headset is recommended, I found the built-in microphones on my Surface tablet and Dell laptop worked well. If necessary, a serviceable plug-in microphone headset for a desktop computer can be bought for a few pounds.

However, it is important to work through the tutorials thoroughly and to spend plenty of time training the computer to recognise your voice. It also helps to speak slowly and clearly into the microphone.

Further Help

In the Control Panel, select **Ease of Access Center** and then **Make touch and tablets easier to use**. The following window opens, including an option for tablet users to choose an accessibility tool (like the Magnifier) to be opened using the Windows Logo button and the Volume Up button on the tablet.

Learn about additional accessibility technologies online at the bottom of the above screenshot is a link to the Microsoft Accessibility Web site. This gives details of products and companies involved in the design of accessibility aids, such as head mounted input devices to overcome physical problems.

Opening the Control Panel

As discussed throughout this book, the Control Panel is used for many important settings. So it may be useful at this point to summarise the various ways you can open the Control Panel.

- Tap or click the **Control Panel** icon on the Apps screen.

- Type the first few letters, such as "**con**", while the Start Screen is displayed or after opening the Search charm.

- In the Desktop screen, select the **Settings** charm, as discussed on page 25, then tap or click **Control Panel** near the top of the right-hand panel on the screen.

- With a mouse, move the cursor to the bottom left-hand corner of the screen and right-click to open the Shortcut Menu shown below. Alternatively, tap and hold in the bottom left-hand corner to display the Shortcut menu. Then tap or click the **Control Panel** option.

The New Start Button in Windows 8.1

In Windows 8.1 the new Start button is displayed in the bottom left-hand corner of the screen. Right-click or tap and hold the Start button to display the Shortcut Menu, shown on the right, with the **Control Panel** highlighted.

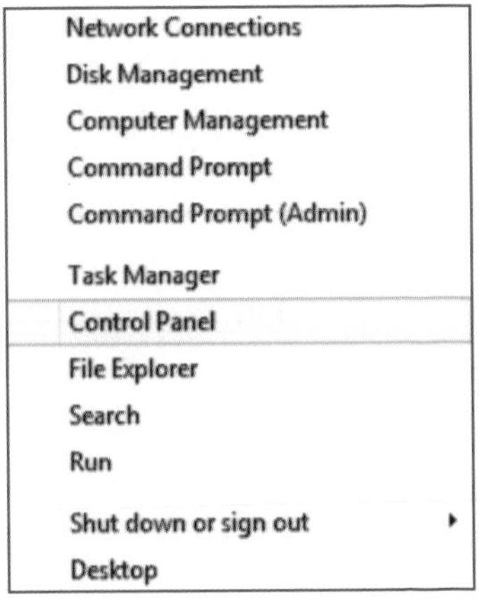

In Windows 8.1, the **File Explorer** is listed in the Shortcut menu as shown on the right. This is also known as the **Windows Explorer** and is used to manage the files and folders stored on your computer and its disc drives. The **Shut down or sign out** option is new in Windows 8.1.

Network Connections

Disk Management

Computer Management

Command Prompt

Command Prompt (Admin)

Task Manager

Control Panel

File Explorer

Search

Run

Shut down or sign out   ▶

Desktop

Getting Connected

Introduction

Whatever type of computer you have — tablet, laptop or desktop machine, the Internet is bound to be a major part of your computing activities. Modern Internet connections use *broadband* technology. This refers to very fast data transfer along special telephone cables. Developments such as fibre optic cables have greatly increased the power of the Internet to download, to your computer, bulky media such as photos, music and video. Here are just a few examples of uses of the Internet.

- Keeping in touch with friends and family anywhere in the world, using e-mail, Skype and social networking websites like Facebook and Twitter. Sharing photos and videos and using live webcams to see people who may be far away.

- Finding the best prices and ordering anything online such as books, holidays and supermarket shopping.

- Buying rail and flight tickets and monitoring actual arrival and departure times in real time.

- Selling surplus goods using the online auction site eBay.

- Searching millions of Web pages to find the latest information on any subject — medical topics, legal advice or hobbies such as gardening or DIY for example.

- Managing your bank accounts and savings online, carrying out major banking transactions. If necessary, filing your Income Tax Self-Assessment online.

- *Downloading* music, videos and apps from the Internet and saving them on your own computer.

Essential Equipment

There are a few things you may need to do before you can start surfing the Internet. It's not difficult and no-one should be put off doing it themselves. The following are the basic requirements:

- A tablet, laptop, or desktop computer with an *Internet adaptor* (or *adapter*) built in or as an add-on accessory.
- An *Internet Access Point* in your home or in a public place such as a hotel or airport.
- An account with an *Internet Service Provider (ISP)*.
- A *Web browser* — a computer program or app which is used to navigate and display Web pages.

Internet Adaptor

New tablet and laptop computers have this Internet connectivity built in during manufacture. On a new computer this feature may need to be switched on. Desktop computers generally need a separate Internet adaptor, often in the form of a *dongle* as shown on the right.

The dongle plugs into one of the small rectangular *USB ports* i.e. connecting sockets, on the computer casing.

Internet Access Point

For the home user this normally means a *wireless router* as shown on the right. This is a device which connects to the Internet, usually via a cable which plugs into a telephone socket in your home. Your computer's Internet adaptor transmits and receives data to and from the router using radio waves.

In our house we have a mixture of tablet, laptop and desktop machines scattered about different rooms and in the home office in the garden. All of them can connect to the Internet via the router, often at the same time.

Wireless networks and technology are often referred to as *WiFi*. Most home networks are now wireless although you can connect a computer to a router using a special *Ethernet* cable. This may be necessary during the initial setting up process.

Network Security

A neighbour with a WiFi computer might detect your network and, without suitable security measures, might access your data. For this reason the router usually has a *password* printed on the back. The password must be entered the first time you go online to the Internet via the router.

Mobile Broadband

Some of the mobile phone networks such as T-Mobile and Orange (both part of EE), enable you to connect your computer to the Internet using *Mobile Broadband*. So you can go online wherever there is a signal for the mobile phone network. Mobile Broadband computers connect using a special USB dongle instead of the router used on home networks. This dongle is similar in size and appearance to the Internet adaptor shown on the previous page. The mobile broadband dongle contains a SIM card to connect the computer to the Internet. Some tablet computers connect to the Internet using a SIM card inserted directly into a special slot in the tablet's casing.

While mobile broadband is particularly useful for computing on the move using a tablet or laptop computer, a mobile broadband dongle can also be used on a desktop computer in a situation where no broadband telephone landline is available. Many hotels, restaurants, trains and airports provide Internet access points. Some organisations offer a free WiFi connection while others make a charge. In some places you may need to ask for a password to enter before you can go online.

Internet Service Providers (ISPs)

As discussed previously, the main methods of connecting to the Internet are by using a router plugged into the telephone socket in your home or via one of the mobile phone networks. Several ISPs provide a broadband service over the BT telephone landlines including BT themselves. You need to go online and look at the various offers before signing up for a contract. If you don't yet have Internet access perhaps you can get help from a friend or relative. Alternatively use a computer in your local library and do a search for **broadband** or **mobile broadband**.

		Bestsellers	Speed	Downloads	Contract	Monthly Cost
1		Three Mobile Broadband 15GB - USB Stick Free Huawei USB modem stick in black incorporating HSPA+ technology - 40% faster than previous models USWITCH.COM BESTSELLER! More info..	up to* **21Mb**	15GB	**24** months	£15.99 Buy now ▸ 0808 163 8657

Once you've signed up for a contract, if using a telephone landline, within a few days the line will be activated for broadband. If you live in an area with the latest *fibre optic* cables you can receive extremely fast broadband such as *BT Infinity*. Your Internet Service Provider may provide a free router and all the necessary accessories, software and passwords. If necessary the ISP may provide an engineer to set the router up for you. Finally the tablet, laptop or desktop computer(s) are connected wirelessly to the router using the wireless adaptor built in or attached to each computer. This is discussed shortly.

If you are connecting a computer to a mobile phone network you can either use pay-as-you-go or take out a contract. It should just be a case of plugging in the dongle or SIM card and launching your Web browser such as Internet Explorer.

Setting up a router and mobile broadband are discussed in more detail in "Basic Computing for the Older Generation– Windows 8 & RT Edition" ISBN 9780859347426 from Bernard Babani (publishing) Ltd.

The Web Browser

Windows 8 uses the Internet Explorer 10 Web browser, while Windows 8.1 uses Internet Explorer 11. A Web browser allows you to find, display and navigate between Web pages. The browser also keeps a list of favourite Web sites. Internet Explorer appears as a tile on the Start Screen as shown on the right.

Tap or click the Internet Explorer tile to start surfing the Internet. Enter the *keywords* for the search, such as **green woodpecker**, for example, into the **bing** search bar, as shown below.

WEB	IMAGES	VIDEOS	MAPS	NEWS	MORE		BING APP

bing   green woodpecker   🔍

1,080,000 RESULTS   Narrow by language ▾   Narrow by region ▾

The RSPB: **Green woodpecker**
www.rspb.org.uk/wildlife/birdguide/name/g/greenwoodpecker/index.asp ▾
Our largest **woodpecker** spends most of its time on the ground, hunting for ants. Did you know that Professor Yaffle (from Bagpuss) was a **green woodpecker**?

Or enter a Web address such as **www.babanibooks.com** into the black address bar at the bottom of the screen. These topics are discussed in more detail in the next chapter.

Although Internet Explorer includes the Bing *search engine*, many people use the freely available Google program, as discussed in the next chapter.

The Internet Explorer Web browser is included in Microsoft Windows by default. Some people believe this gives Microsoft and Internet Explorer an unfair advantage over other browsers. While the general user should find Internet Explorer meets their browsing needs, some advanced users prefer to use alternatives such as Google Chrome or Mozilla Firefox.

Making the Connection

This section describes the steps needed to connect a computer to a WiFi network. This might be a wireless router in your home or an access point in a public place such as a hotel or restaurant, etc. Each computer must have an Internet adaptor and Web browser software. If necessary the Internet connectivity in a tablet or laptop should be switched on. In the case of a home network, the router should be connected by a cable to a telephone line which has been activated for broadband by an Internet Service Provider such as BT. The router connects to the telephone socket through a *filter* which has two sockets, one for the router and one for the telephone handset. This allows the Internet and an ordinary telephone to be used at the same time.

Detecting the Router or Internet Access Point

Switch on the computer and enter your password to open the Start Screen. Swipe in from the right edge or click in the bottom right-hand corner of the screen to display the Charms Bar, as discussed in Chapter 2. Then tap or click the **Settings** charm shown on the right. You should see the following displayed at the bottom right of the screen.

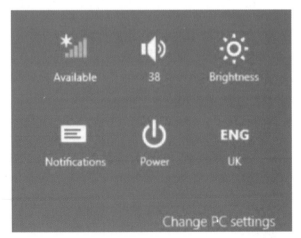

The WiFi icon shown on the right and on the top left of the previous screenshot indicates that network connections are available. In the home situation this should include your router and possibly some of your neighbours' networks if they are within the WiFi range. Depending on  your equipment, this might be up to 150 feet indoors or 300 feet outdoors. An Internet access point in a public place would be detected in a similar way. Tap or click the icon shown above to list the available networks, as shown below.

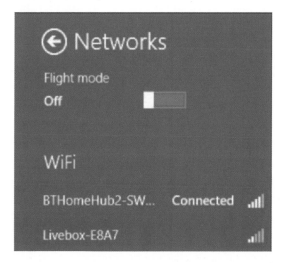

In the example above, **BTHomeHub2-SW...** is our own BT router while **Livebox-E8A7** belongs to a neighbour. These routers must be up and running and within WiFi range. **Flight mode** above must be **Off** to connect to the Internet. It is switched on and off by tapping or clicking the small rectangle shown above next to **Off**. Flight mode **On** prevents the transmission of radio signals, which could interfere with an aircraft's systems. With Flight mode **On** you can still use the computer for non-Internet activities like music or word processing.

Connecting to the Router

Tap or click the name of your router in the list of routers, similar to the list on the previous page. You are then asked for a *security key*, often a string of numbers and letters stamped or printed on the back of the router. Without the protection of the security key anyone within WiFi range could detect and connect to your router and possibly access the information on any of the computers on your home network. For this reason you should always use a router which requires a security key.

After selecting your own router and entering the security key, tap or click **Connect** to complete the Internet connection. There is also a box to tick if you wish to connect to the Internet automatically at the start of every computing session. The word **Connected** now appears against your chosen router, as shown on the right.

Now, whenever you select the **Settings** charm, the name of your router, **BTHomeHub2-SW8N** in this example, should appear as shown on the right and below.

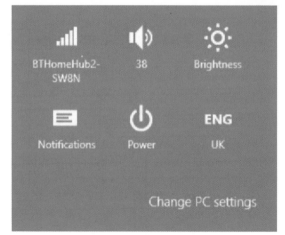

Troubleshooting

After using routers and network adaptors for a number of years, we have had very few problems in setting up the equipment or with the reliability of the connections to the Internet. However, you may suffer the odd glitch from time to time. This is indicated by the **Unavailable** note and white cross in a red circle on the WiFi icon as shown on the right.

Possible causes of this problem are:

- Some computers have an Internet switch and this may be turned off. This may be a physical switch. On my laptop the F2 function key is used as the Internet switch.

- The computer may use an Internet adaptor in the form of a USB dongle and there may be a bad connection or the adaptor is unplugged.

- **Flight mode**, as discussed earlier, is turned **On** in the **Settings** feature. Flight mode prevents Internet access.

- The cables between the router, the filter and the telephone socket are not properly connected.

- There may be a problem with the telephone line between your home and the telephone exchange. The further you are from the exchange, the weaker the broadband signal.

- Your Internet Service Provider may be carrying out maintenance work on their network.

- If you are upgrading to Windows 8.1 from an earlier version such as Windows XP, you might find some compatibility problems. If your computer has a network adaptor dongle you might find (as we did) that your Windows XP network adaptor is not compatible with Windows 8.1.

Overcoming Internet Connection Problems

Here are a few suggestions if you have trouble making the connection to the Internet:

- Make sure the Internet switch on your computer is in the **On** position (if applicable).

- Check that **Flight mode** is switched off.

- Check your router's handbook. The diagnostic lights should tell you if the broadband and WiFi are working.

- Router problems can often be solved by switching the router off and then switching it back on.

- Similarly, if you are using a network adaptor dongle, try removing the dongle for a short time before refitting it.

- Check that all cables are correctly connected.

- If you have a plug-in wireless network adaptor, make sure it is compatible with Windows 8.1. (Windows 7 adaptors should work with Windows 8.1). A new network adaptor dongle can be bought for a few pounds.

You can see what network adaptor is fitted to your computer (even if it is built-in during manufacture) by opening the Control Panel, as discussed on page 48. This can be done quickly from the Start Screen by typing the first few letters such as **con** then tapping or  clicking **Control Panel** in the rectangle on the top right of the screen, as shown on the right above.

Then select **Hardware and Sound**, **Device Manager** and **Network adaptors**.

Our wireless network adaptor is listed below.

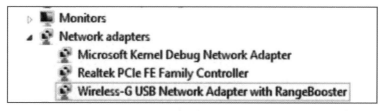

If you tap twice or double-click the name of your adaptor, you can find more information about the adaptor and its status — working or otherwise. If necessary download the latest software *drivers* to make it work with Windows 8.1.

Internet Speed

The various Internet Service Providers include broadband speed in their advertisements. The figures quoted are usually the *download* speeds for transmitting data from the Internet to your computer. This is particularly important if you want to download large files such as videos, photo collections and music and for streaming "catchup" television using BBC iPlayer, etc.

Broadband speed is usually quoted in *megabits per second* or *Mbps* or simply *Mb*. (Bits are binary digits, the 0s and 1s used to represent letters, etc., in the computer.) The minimum download speed for a service to be classed as broadband is 2Mb. Typical broadband speeds advertised at the time of writing range from 8 to 70Mb. In practice your actual speed may be considerably less.

The actual broadband speed achieved depends on a number of factors. Some remote areas of Britain can't receive broadband at all, while others have the very latest fibre optic cables. Distance from your telephone exchange is also a factor. In the future, fibre cables from the exchange to the cabinet (often green) in your road (FTTC) promise speeds of up to 40 Mb. In the longer term, fibre cables from the telephone exchange all the way to your home (FTTH) are forecast to give speeds of 100Mb or more.

Checking Your Broadband Speed

Type "**Broadband speed**" or similar into a search program such as Bing or Google. You'll find several links to speed test programs. These measure your download and upload speeds. The results of a test on our broadband service are shown below.

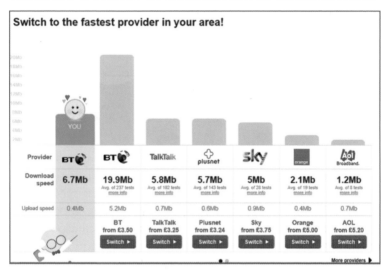

As shown above in the green **YOU** column on the extreme left, our download speed is 6.7Mb, in line with the British average of 7Mb. The uSwitch speed test above also gives details of alternative broadband services in our area. As shown above, it appears that a BT service of 20Mb is available in our road. This is the BT Infinity fibre optic service and although we live near to the telephone exchange our road doesn't have the necessary fibre cables. You can check the maximum BT broadband speed you can receive by opening the BT Web site **at www.bt.com** and entering your telephone number in the BT Infinity section.

Broadband option	Broadband speed range	Earliest you could get it
BT Total Broadband ⑦	Between 7.5Mb and 17.5Mb (Estimated speed: 13.0Mb)	Now

Connecting Printers

Previous pages have shown how a single wireless router can be used to connect one or more computers to the Internet using wireless technology. The computers can also be set up to "see" other computers on the home network and transfer files such as text documents and photographs. Once set up, this is quicker than alternative file transfer methods such as copying them to a removable flash drive or e-mailing the files to yourself.

Similarly the wireless home network can be used to allow several computers scattered around your home to send output to a single printer. Or you can have more than one printer on the home network and select whichever is best for the job in hand.

Detecting a Printer

If you are setting up a printer for the first time, it needs to be connected to a computer using a USB cable. If it is a wireless printer the cable may still be needed during the initial setup process. When connecting a computer to a printer on a wireless network, the printer needs to be online, up and running and not in *sleep mode*.

Open the **Control Panel** as discussed on page 48. From the **Control Panel** select the green heading **Hardware and Sound**. On the next window select **Advanced printer setup** under **Devices and Printers**.

Windows then searches for available printers. If it finds more than one, select the printer you wish to connect to and then tap or click **Next**.

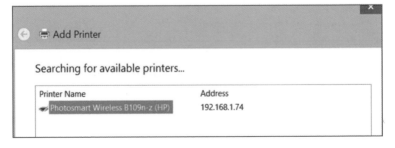

Windows will then search the Internet for the necessary *device* drivers, i.e. software to enable the printer to work with Windows 8.1. It may be necessary for you to use the CD or DVD which came with the printer or to log on to the printer manufacturer's Web site and download a suitable driver.

All being well you should see a note like the following, giving you the chance to print a test page.

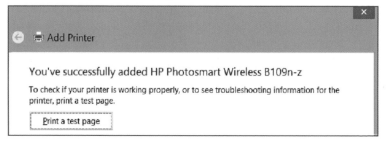

Select **Finish** and the printer should be ready to use.

To check on your printer at any time, select **Control Panel/ Hardware and Sound/View Devices and Printers**. The printer icon with a tick against it is the default printer. This will be used automatically whenever you print from within a program, such as Microsoft Word or Excel.

The **Devices and Printers** window can be used to check on the status of a printer and cancel any troublesome print jobs. Press and hold or right-click the printer icon to display a shortcut printer menu. This includes changing the default printer. Double tap or double click the printer icon to display printer status information.

Using the Internet

Introduction

Internet Explorer is a *Web browser*, an app, i.e. program, used to navigate the enormous number of pages of information stored on millions of computers around the world. The Internet Explorer Web browser has for many years been supplied with the Microsoft Windows operating system, used in the majority of computers in the world. Manufacturers of rival Web browsers felt this gave Microsoft an unfair advantage. As a result Microsoft have been forced to offer a *Browser Choice Window* delivered through Windows Update and allowing you to install alternative Web browsers such as Google Chrome and Mozilla Firefox.

Internet Explorer has been used by many millions of people over the years and the latest editions have been well received, being very fast and with many innovative features. Windows 8 and RT use Internet Explorer 10 while Windows 8.1 and RT 8.1 use Internet Explorer 11.

Some of the main functions of a Web browser are:

- To display Web pages containing specified information, after you enter keywords into a *search engine* (a program) such as bing or Google.

- To open Web sites after their unique addresses are typed into the Address Bar in the browser.

- To navigate between different Web pages using *hyperlinks*, i.e. clickable or tappable links in the pages and also using *forward* and *back* buttons and *tabs*.

- To save links or *bookmarks* allowing you to return to *favourite* or recently visited Web sites.

The Keyword Search

Using the bing Search Engine

The range of subjects and depth of information available on the Internet is amazing. In my experience you can find up-to-date information on virtually any subject under the sun. For example, suppose you want to find out about the red squirrel. From the Start Screen tap or click the **Internet Explorer** tile, shown on the right.

Then enter **red squirrel** in the bing search bar, as shown below.

When you tap or click the **Web Search** button shown above you will see a list of search results almost instantly, as shown below.

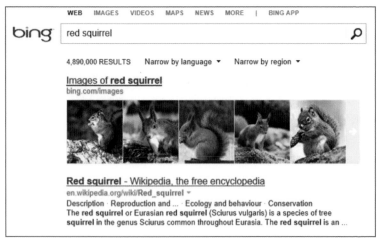

To look at a Web page, tap or click its blue link in the list of search results, such as **Images of red squirrel** above.

The New Search Feature in Windows 8.1

Open the **Search** charm as discussed on page 23. If using a keyboard, with the Start Screen displayed, start typing the keyword (s) for the search. When you tap or click the magnifying glass search icon or press the Enter

key, the results are presented as shown below.

As shown above, instead of a list of brief details, as produced by previous methods of searching in bing and Google, the new search feature displays miniature versions of the Web pages found in the search. These give more information than the list of results shown on the previous page. The miniature Web pages shown above are links to the full size Web sites.

Only a small sample of the results found for **red squirrel** are shown above. To see all the results, scroll horizontally by swiping with a touch screen or dragging if using a mouse.

Upper and Lower Case Letters in Keywords

samuel johnson yields the same results as **Samuel Johnson** or even **SAMUEL JOHNSON**.

Narrowing a Search Using Inverted Commas

Entering **"red squirrel"** will eliminate unwanted results, such as a page containing "a grey **squirrel** was eating **red** berries".

The Google Search Engine

Google has been the leading search engine for many years. It is free and can be opened by entering **www.google.co.uk** into the Address Bar at the bottom of the Internet Explorer screen.

The Google Search Bar appears as shown below, ready for you to enter keywords to search the Web.

The icon shown on the right and in context below appears at the top right of the Google screen.

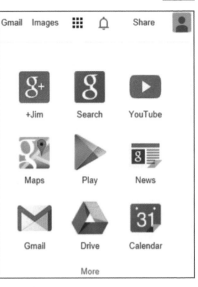

Tap or click this icon to display the Google features shown on the right. You can, for example, search **YouTube** for videos, select **Play** to search for Apps in the Google Play Store and tap or click **News** to see the latest headlines. **Drive** is the storage space in the "clouds" which Google allocates for you to save your files in. Also shown is an icon for **Gmail,** the Google e-mail system. **Images**, shown above, produces search results in the form of pictures, for a particular subject.

Using a Web Address

Most companies, organisations and many individuals now have their own Web site, to publish news and information. Each Web site is identified on the Internet by a unique address or *URL* (*Uniform Resource Locator*). Many organisations include their address on their correspondence or on their vehicles, for example:

www.babanibooks.com

The Web address gives a very quick way to move directly to a particular Web site, without having to peruse a list of search results, as with the keyword search.

From the Start Screen shown on page 71, tap or click the Internet tile, as shown on the right. The Internet Explorer Home Page opens, as shown in the example below. For normal browsing the Web page occupies the whole of the screen. However, if you swipe up from the bottom or  down from the top, or right click a mouse, the black Address Bar appears across the bottom of the screen, as shown below.

Tap or click the Address Bar at the bottom of the screen and enter the new Web address to replace the previous one, as shown below.

When you tap or press **Enter**, the required Web site is quickly displayed.

Navigating Around a Web Site

Within most Web pages there are numerous *links* or *hyperlinks*, usually in the form of text or images. If you pass a cursor over a link, the cursor changes to a hand. Tapping or clicking the link opens another page on the Web site or opens another Web site. Circled arrows at the extreme left and right of the Address Bar, as shown for Windows 8 and Windows RT below, allow you to move forward and back through previously visited pages.

As shown on the right, the Windows 8.1 and RT 8.1 Address Bar is slightly different  from the Address Bar in Windows 8. The functions of the various icons are described on the next page.

Windows 8 and RT and Windows 8.1 and RT 8.1

 This icon refreshes the Web page with the latest up-to-date information.

 Tapping or clicking this icon displays options to pin a tile for the current Web page on the Start Screen or on Favorites, as discussed shortly.

 This icon has options to search for and highlight certain words in a long document. You can also view a Web page in the traditional Windows Desktop

Windows 8.1 and RT 8.1 Only

 This icon displays tabs or small thumbnails of previously visited Web sites, enabling you to switch between Web sites very quickly, as discussed on the next page.

 This opens the Favorites Bar shown below. The star icon on the right adds a Web site  to the Favorites Bar, shown below. The middle icon pins a Web site to the Start Screen, as discussed above. The right-hand icon allows you to share a Web page with friends.

The Favorites Bar — Windows 8.1 and RT 8.1

Tapping or clicking a tile on the Favorites Bar allows you to return to a previously visited Web site.

Tabbed Browsing

With a Web site open in Internet Explorer, swipe in from the top or bottom or right-click a mouse. Tap or click the **New Tab** icon shown on the right and on the top right on the main screenshot below.

Now open another Web site either by a keyword search or by entering its address in the Address Bar of Internet Explorer, as discussed earlier in this chapter. The new Web site opens with its own tab, as shown below.

In Windows 8 & RT, the tabs are displayed along the top of the screen, as shown in the above screenshots. In Windows 8.1 and RT 8.1, the thumbnails appear along the bottom of the screen.

To switch between Web sites simply tap or click the tab or thumbnail image of the page. To close a Web site tap or click the cross on the tab.

The Windows Store

When you first begin using Windows 8.1, the Start Screen already displays a lot of tiles, representing apps or programs. These are included by default in a new installation of Windows 8.1. As discussed earlier, you may also have tiles for apps and Web sites which you have pinned to the Start Screen yourself.

The default tiles include popular apps such as News, Weather, Internet Explorer, People, SkyDrive, Camera, Skype, Mail, Maps, Photos, the Desktop, Music and Video. In addition the Store tile allows you to browse thousands of apps which have been specially designed to work with the Modern UI (User Interface) including the Start Screen in Windows 8.1, as shown above. Apps are available in a wide variety of categories such as health, music, entertainment, education, business, sport, books, food and lifestyle. New apps are continually being designed and added to the Store. Many apps are free to download and install on your computer, while others may cost a few pounds.

When you download an app, you become the owner of that app. If necessary, use the Pin to Start icon shown on pages 68 and 69 to place a tile for the app on your Start Screen. You may be allowed to install an app on up to 5 different computers.

The Windows Store is opened by tapping or clicking its tile on the Start Screen as shown on the right. Then you can scroll through thousands of apps, some listed under headings representing broad categories such as **News & Weather** or **Sport**.

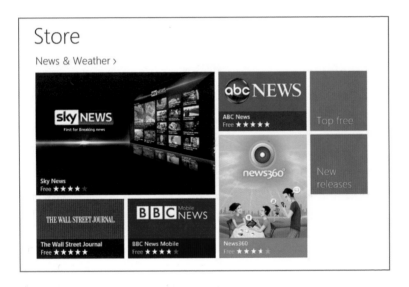

Other tiles in the Windows Store represent a single app, such as the well-known Google search engine and the online auction house eBay. There is also an app for the free Skype Internet telephone service, discussed later in this book. These new apps make it easier to use the services from within the Modern UI. Sample tiles for some well-known apps in the Windows Store are shown below.

The range of apps covers most aspects of life, such as help with medical matters in the **Health Choices** app, which gives information about NHS services.

Downloading and Installing an App

Although the Amazon Kindle is well-known as a leading tablet for reading books electronically, you can download a Kindle app for use on other computers. This turns your Windows 8.1 tablet, laptop or desktop computer into an e-book reader. Scroll through the Windows Store to find the **Books & Reference** section. Tap or click **Books & Reference** and then select **Kindle**, as shown on the right and on the lower right below.

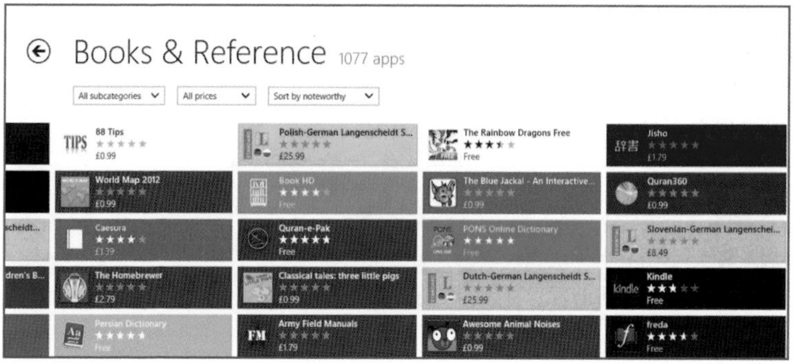

You are then presented with a description of the app, as follows.

Now tap or click **Install**, shown above. If there is a charge for the app you will have to supply your name and address and credit card details, etc. The app is downloaded to your computer in a few seconds and a tile appears on your Start Screen. In this example, the tile for the new Kindle app is shown on the right, together with three other newly installed apps from the Windows Store. Tap or click the tile on the Start Screen to launch the Kindle app, as shown below.

Internet Security

By enabling millions of computers to communicate with each other around the world, the Internet has created opportunities in work, education, communication and entertainment, etc., that previous generations could never have imagined. Unfortunately, in addition to these legitimate activities, the Internet provides skilful *hackers* with opportunities for a range of criminal acts. Unlike conventional crime, there is no burglary or violence and the criminal may be thousands of miles from the crime scene — which might be the computer in your home.

A major type of Internet crime is *malware*, i.e. malicious software. This is the use of specially written programs designed to damage or invade your computer and its files. These include *viruses*, *worms* and *Trojan horses*. Viruses may be attached to e-mails or software and are designed to spread, cause damage to files and slow down computer systems and networks. Worms can spread without being attached to a program. The Trojan Horse poses as a legitimate piece of software but has an illegal purpose such as to give a hacker access to your computer. *Spyware* uses *phishing* to try to find out personal and financial information, such as your bank account details.

Windows 8.1 provide a wide range of security software to combat these threats. These are turned on by default but it's worth checking they are up and running and up-to-date.

Open the Control Panel, as discussed on page 48, and under **System and Security**, select **Review your computer's status**. In the **Action Center** shown below, tap or click the arrow to the right of the word **Security**.

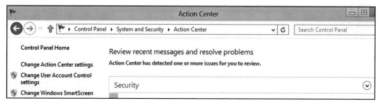

This displays a drop-down list of the main security tools and their status, **On** or **Off**, as shown below.

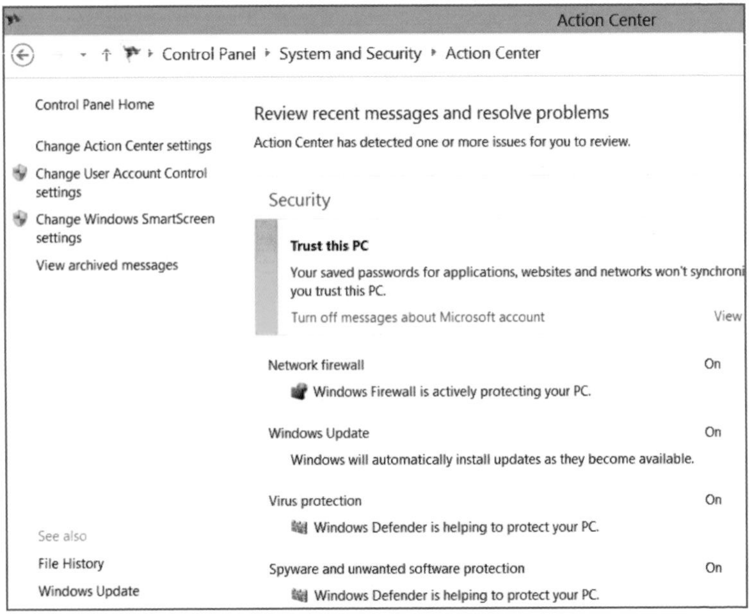

To change the **On** or **Off** status of any of the security messages, tap or click **Change Action Center settings** shown at the top left of the **Action Center** shown above. Then tap or click the check box to add or remove a tick from a security tool.

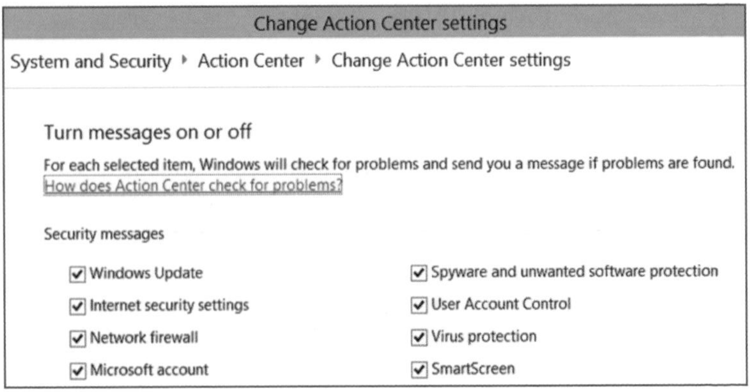

Windows Firewall

The **Windows Firewall** shown on the previous page is a barrier designed to stop hackers and malicious software such as worms from entering your computer. The firewall can also prevent malware being sent out from a computer to the Internet.

Windows Update

Windows Update downloads and installs the latest software upgrades from Microsoft, frequently intended to fix security problems. This is usually done automatically or you may be asked to choose whether or not to install an update. The Browser Choice window (discussed earlier) may be downloaded as a Windows Update. A log of all your recent updates is kept in the **update history** shown below. This is displayed after selecting **Windows Update** at the bottom left of the **Action Center** shown at the top of the previous page. Then tap or click **View update history** at the top left of the **Windows Update** window.

	View update history		
← ・ ↑ ■ ▸ Control Panel ▸ System and Security ▸ Windows Update ▸ View update history			
Review your update history			
Check the Status column to ensure all important updates were successful. To remove an update, see Installed Updates.			
Troubleshoot problems with installing updates			
Name	Status	Importance	Date installed
Definition Update for Windows Defender - KB2267602 (Definition 1.141.645.0)	Succeeded	Important	28/11/2012
Definition Update for Windows Defender - KB2267602 (Definition 1.141.523.0)	Succeeded	Important	27/11/2012
Definition Update for Windows Defender - KB2267602 (Definition 1.141.419.0)	Succeeded	Important	26/11/2012
Definition Update for Windows Defender - KB2267602 (Definition 1.141.354.0)	Succeeded	Important	24/11/2012
Definition Update for Windows Defender - KB2267602 (Definition 1.141.218.0)	Succeeded	Important	22/11/2012
Definition Update for Windows Defender - KB2267602 (Definition 1.141.135.0)	Succeeded	Important	21/11/2012
Definition Update for Windows Defender - KB2267602 (Definition 1.141.7.0)	Succeeded	Important	20/11/2012
Definition Update for Windows Defender - KB2267602 (Definition 1.139.2352.0)	Succeeded	Important	19/11/2012
Update for Windows RT (KB2769165)	Succeeded	Important	18/11/2012

Many of the updates downloaded by Windows Update are *virus definitions*. These allow anti-virus software such as the Windows Defender to detect and eradicate the latest viruses. The Defender is listed in the Action Center at the top of the previous page and discussed on the next page.

Windows Defender

This software is included in Windows 8.1 and should always be switched **On**, as previously discussed. The **Windows Defender** window shown below can be quickly launched from its icon on the Apps screen, shown on the right. The Apps screen can be opened as discussed on  page 7. Then scroll across the Apps screen and tap or click the **Windows Defender** icon shown above.

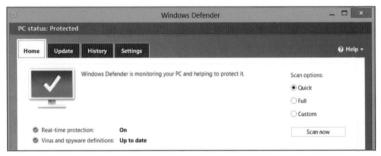

Windows Defender continually monitors your computer for viruses, spyware and malware. You can also launch a manual scan whenever you wish, using **Scan now** shown in the bottom right-hand corner above. Viruses are continually being developed, so the latest virus and spyware definitions are regularly updated and automatically included in Defender.

SmartScreen

The SmartScreen shown on page 76 detects suspicious e-mails, etc., from unknown sources which can't be detected by normal antimalware. The SmartScreen Filter issues alerts about unsafe Web sites which may be "phishing" for your bank details, etc.

Electronic Mail

This was one of the first popular applications of the Internet and remains extremely important in both social and business situations. Although *social networking* Web sites like Facebook and Twitter (discussed in the next chapter) provide exciting new methods of communication, *e-mail* has some advantages.

E-mail replaces the letter sent in the post between friends, family and business contacts. Some advantages of e-mail are:

- The message is delivered to its destination almost instantly. It is then immediately available to be read.
- The same message can be sent to many recipients, easily selected from an electronic address book.
- It is very simple for recipients to *reply* or *forward* the message to someone else.
- An e-mail can have files attached, such as text documents (like this chapter), spreadsheets, videos or photographs.
- Messages can easily be deleted or saved in an organised structure of folders, for future reference.
- E-mail can be used for long messages. Social networks like Twitter are limited to very short messages.

Electronic mail might be used to communicate with long-lost relatives around the world, including the exchange of photographs. Documents, photographs and other files are "clipped" (metaphorically speaking) to the message and are known as *attachments*. The text in the main body of the e-mail can be quite lengthy or it may simply be a covering note for any attachments. If you want a friend to see a particular Web site, you can embed a *link* to the Web site in the e-mail. Your friend simply taps or clicks the link to launch the Web site.

The Windows Mail App

The e-mail app in Windows 8.1 is known as *Windows Mail* or simply *Mail*. This is launched by tapping or clicking its tile on the Start Screen, shown on the left of the extract below.

In the example below, I have sent a test e-mail to myself. The **1** at the bottom right of the tile is a *notification* of a new message.

Tap or click the tile to open the **Mail** window. The main body of the e-mail is shown below.

Jim Gatenby   Sun 15 Dec 19:29
to Jim Gatenby

Test

You can send a copy of an e-mail to yourself to check what your contact will receive.

Sent from Windows Mail

The E-mail Address

In order to send and receive e-mails you need a unique e-mail address such as:

stellajohnson@hotmail.com

Windows 8.1 uses your Microsoft e-mail address to sign in to the Lock Screen, to access the Windows Store and to share information with sites such as Facebook and Twitter.

Creating a New Microsoft Account

From the **Settings** charm discussed in Chapter 2, select **Change PC settings**. In Windows 8 and RT select **Users** then **Add a user**. In Windows 8.1 and RT 8.1 select **Change PC settings**, **Accounts**, **Other accounts** and **Add an account**.

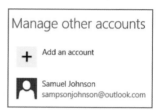

Next you can use an existing address or alternatively click **Sign up for a new e-mail address** to create a new Microsoft account, as shown below.

Enter your chosen name in front of **@outlook.com** shown above. Once you've signed up for a new e-mail address you can start using it to send and receive messages in **Mail**.

If you've had a Microsoft account before (with Windows 7, say), this e-mail address can be used with Mail and other apps in Windows 8.1.

After you've signed in to the Lock Screen discussed in Chapters 2 and 3, tap or click the **Mail** tile on the Start Screen, shown on the right. The **Mail** window opens displaying the **Inbox**, as shown below.

Tap or click **Folders** on the left-hand side to view the **Inbox**, **Drafts**, **Sent**, **Outbox**, **Junk** and **Deleted** folders, etc. Tap or click a folder to open and view the messages.

Receiving an E-mail

The messages you receive are listed in the centre panel of the **Inbox** with the sender's name, subject and time, as shown below. If you highlight a message, three icons appear on the right, as shown below.

The icons on the right above allow you to **Mark as unread**, **Delete** a message or **Flag** the message. You can flag messages as a reminder that they need your attention in the future. If a message has a file *attachment*, a paperclip icon is displayed, as shown on the right below.

| Jim Gatenby | 📎 \| 2 |
| Back Cover | 20:09 |

Tap or click the listing of the message in the Inbox, as shown on the previous page, to open it for reading as shown below.

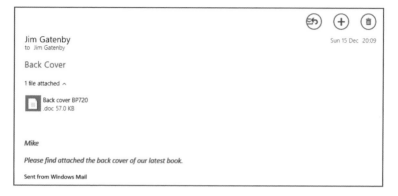

At the top left is the sender's name with the date and time of sending on the right. The name next to **to:** above should be the real recipient's name rather than mine used in this dummy test.

The three icons on the right and also shown above are for responding to a message, starting a new message and deleting a message, as discussed in more detail on page 88.

The Attachment

The icon shown on the right and above is an attachment, in this case a document file produced in the Word program. Tap or click the icon to display a menu with options

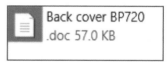

to open or save the file. If you select **Open**, the document will open in its associated program such as Microsoft Word. Similarly a spreadsheet file might open in Microsoft Excel and a drawing or photo might open in Windows Paint. **Open with** lets you choose the program to use. **Save** lets you select a folder on your hard drive or internal storage in which to save the attachment.

Creating an E-mail

To create a new message, tap or click the **Mail** tile on the Start Screen shown earlier. Then tap or click the **New** icon shown on the right and on the previous page.

A new blank e-mail window opens ready for you to enter the text of the message. First enter the e-mail addresses of the main recipients in the **To:** slot, pressing **Enter** after each one.

Jim Gatenby
jimgatenby@hotmail.com ⌄

To	
Cc	
Bcc	

Priority   Normal   ⌄

[Draft] Add a subject

The **Cc:** slot above is used to send a (carbon) copy to other people who may be interested. Anyone included in **Bcc** receives a copy of the message, unknown to the other recipients. In Windows 8.1 tap or click **To, Cc,** or **Bcc** and select recipients from your contacts list which drops down. People are added to your contacts list automatically when you receive their mail.

Next give a title to the message, replacing the words **Add a subject** shown above. It's now time to start entering the main body text below the horizontal line under **Add a subject**, shown above. Swipe in from the top or bottom or right click a mouse to display the formatting toolbar along the bottom of the screen, as shown below. The formatting features include different font styles, sizes and colour of letters and bold and italics, etc.

The above toolbar also appears when you highlight a piece of text.

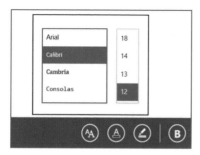 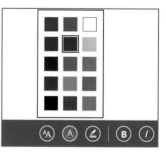

In the example below, the font style, size and colour have been set using the toolbar icons and pop-up menus shown above.

If you tap or click the **Emoticons** icon shown on the right and near the bottom of the previous page, you are presented with images on different subjects to add to the e-mail text, as shown in the small extract below. These allow you to express feelings or add humour to a message.

Inserting an Attachment

If you wish to include a file such as a photo or text document, you need to know where the file has been saved, such as in a folder on your hard disc drive or on a removable flash drive. In Windows 8 and RT, open the Mail toolbar on the bottom of the screen, by swiping in from the top or bottom or right clicking with a mouse. In Windows 8 and RT the **Attachments** icon, shown on the right in the middle, appears on the left of the Taskbar, at the bottom of the screen.

In Windows 8.1 and RT 8.1, the **Attachments** icon is again in the form of a paperclip as shown on the right, but this now appears at the top right of the screen.

Tap or click the **Attachments** icon to open the **Files** window and browse your computer and its discs, flash drives, etc., for the required file.

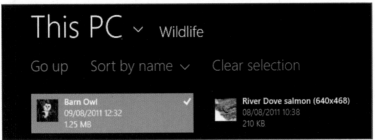

When you tap or click to select a file to send with your e-mail, the file is ticked, as shown above and the **Attach** button at the bottom right of the screen is highlighted, as shown on the right. Tap or click the **Attach** button and an icon or thumbnail image of the document or photo appears on the left of the e-mail message, as shown on the next page.

Sending an E-mail

The finished e-mail, complete with recipients' e-mail addresses, subject, body text and any attachments can now be sent by tapping or clicking the envelope icon shown on the right and near the top right of the message window above. A copy of the message is temporarily placed in your **Outbox** until it has been actually sent. Then it will appear in your **Sent** folder as shown below.

Responding to an E-mail

New messages are listed in the centre panel of your Inbox, with the sender's name, day or time and a paperclip icon if there are any attachments, as shown below.

Tap or click the e-mail header shown above to open the message and then tap or click the attachment thumbnail or icon.

Then select **Open, Open with** or **Save** from the menu shown above. In this example, **Open with** was selected to open a photo in the Windows Paint program, shown on the right. **Save** allows you to store a copy of the document or photo on your computer's hard disc drive, etc.

To send a reply to an e-mail, tap or click the **Respond** icon on the left of the three icons shown on the right and on the previous page. **Reply** sends your reply to the original sender. **Reply all** sends your reply to the original sender and to everyone who received the

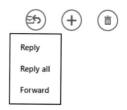

original message. Their e-mail addresses are entered automatically — you only need to enter the text of your reply. **Forward** is used to send on a copy of the original message to someone you think might be interested.

Using SkyDrive to Share Files

SkyDrive gives you 7GB of free storage in the *clouds*. This storage space is, in fact, on Microsoft's server computers connected via the Internet to create a *data warehouse*. With all your data files stored on SkyDrive, you can access them from any computer in the world, after signing on with your username and password. To share a document or photo, etc., with someone else, instead of sending an e-mail attachment, you send them an e-mail which includes a *link*. They simply tap or click the link to open the file from SkyDrive. Bigger files can be shared using SkyDrive than can be sent as e-mail attachments.

Uploading Files to SkyDrive

There is a SkyDrive app with a tile on the Start Screen, as shown on the right. To send a file to SkyDrive, tap or click the icon on the Start Screen. Then tap or click to open the folder on SkyDrive where the file is to be stored. Now right-click or

swipe up from the bottom to display the Taskbar at the bottom of the screen. Then tap or click **Add files** shown on the right and browse, as

shown on page 86, to locate and select the required file.

After selecting one or more files, tap or click the **Copy to SkyDrive** button at the bottom right of the screen.

Alternatively, open the File Explorer, as shown on the right. Then use *copy* and *paste* or *drag* and *drop* to copy files onto the SkyDrive folder (if available).

Sending a Link Via E-mail

Log onto SkyDrive at: **https://skydrive.live.com**. In SkyDrive, find the file you want to share, as shown on the right, and tap and hold or right click the icon for the file. Then select **Share with** and **SkyDrive** from the drop-down menu which appears. The Window shown below opens for you enter the e-mail address of the recipient(s) who are to be sent a link to the file. You

can add a short note, if you wish. On receiving your e-mail a recipient simply taps or clicks the link to open and possibly edit the file.

Share	Invite people to this photo
Invite people	Enter contacts to send an email to with a link to this item.
Get a link	To
Publish to	
Shared with	Add a quick note
Only me	
	Recipients can only view
	Share Close

Social Networking

Introduction

As discussed in the previous chapter, electronic mail was for many years the main method of communication between people using the Internet. However, recent years have seen the arrival of *social networking* Web sites, designed to provide new ways for people to interact and exchange information. Some of the most popular free Web sites used for social networking, which have millions of users worldwide, are as follows:

Facebook

Users enter biographical information, including a Timeline of major life events. They may then become friends with like-minded people to exchange news and photographs, etc.

Twitter

This Web site allows you to post short text messages on the Internet. Users can choose to follow the messages of other people such as friends, family and celebrities. Twitter can also be used for online debates on popular subjects and causes.

LinkedIn

Professional people use this Web site to build up their contacts lists, to find out about employment opportunities and to provide prospective employers with their CVs, etc.

Skype

Although not a social networking Web site like Facebook and Twitter, Skype allows people to communicate, using free voice and video calls between computers, anywhere on the Internet.

The People App

The People app in Windows 8.1 is designed to integrate all your social networking contacts and has a tile on the Start Screen. The tile is a constantly changing  display of images from your Facebook, Twitter and e-mail contacts, as shown above on the right. The People app collects together all of the people you interact with on the Internet, on Facebook, Twitter, Email, Skype, etc. and sorts them into an alphabetical list. Tap or click the **People** tile to display the list, as shown in the extract below.

Connected to

People What's new Me			
James Gatenby	John Gatenby	Mike Brunt	richardg1976@r
jamesfoulds@safe...	john@copperbee...	O	S
Jill Gatenby	L	Olivia Kemps	stella austin
jillgatenby@hotm...	London Eating	R	stella jill gatenb
jmbrunt@waitros...	London Symphon...	reservations@par...	stellaaustin@liv

Tap or click **What's new** shown above to see a list of your friends' latest updates on Facebook or Twitter.

Launching Facebook and Twitter — Web Site or App

You can launch Facebook and Twitter in Windows 8.1 by logging on to their Web sites. Alternatively, there are apps in the Windows Store for Facebook and Twitter. The Twitter app can be used with Windows 8 and RT and Windows 8.1 and RT 8.1. The Facebook app can be used with Windows 8.1 and RT 8.1, but not with Windows 8 and RT. To run the Facebook app, Windows 8 and RT users need to upgrade to Windows 8.1 or RT 8.1.

Introducing Facebook

This is probably the most popular social networking site, with over a billion users. Although originally started by college students in America, it's now used by people of all ages. Facebook is becoming increasingly popular with older people, especially if they have children and grandchildren on the other side of the world. Businesses and celebrities also use Facebook for promotional purposes.

Facebook Friends

Facebook is based around the concept of having lots of *friends*. These may include close personal friends and family but may also include people you have never met in the real world. Some people have thousands of "friends" on Facebook.

These virtual friends are people with whom you've agreed to share news and information across the Internet. Facebook identifies people who you might want to invite to be your friends, perhaps because they are in the list of contacts in your e-mail address book and are already members of Facebook. When you join Facebook you can enter a personal profile giving details of your education, employment and interests, etc. This information allows Facebook to suggest people who you might want to invite to be a friend. They can either accept or decline this invitation.

Confidentiality and Security

Facebook provides a platform for you to post a great deal of personal and biographical information on the Internet. The Internet enables this information to be viewed by a potential audience of millions of people. Facebook has privacy settings, known as *audience selectors*, to allow you to restrict the viewing of certain types of information to specific groups of people. It's advisable not to put confidential information on Facebook unless you're thoroughly conversant with the privacy settings. You are also advised not to accept complete strangers as Facebook friends or arrange to meet up with them.

Using Facebook from the Web Site

This page describes the opening of Facebook from the Facebook Web site rather than using an app from the Windows Store. First open Internet Explorer from its tile on the Start Screen. Launch **Facebook** by typing the Web address, i.e. **www.facebook.com**, into the address bar, as previously described. Then swipe in from the top or bottom or right click with the mouse, to display the toolbar shown below. As described on pages 68 and 69, there are slight differences in the toolbar icons between Windows 8 and 8.1 (similarly Windows RT and RT 8.1), but the general methods for creating Web site tiles are the same.

Tap or click the pin icon, shown on the right and above, to open the small window shown on the left below. Tap or click **Pin to Start**, shown below, to place a tile for Facebook on the Start Screen, as shown on the right.

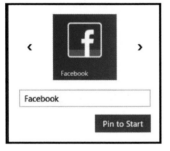

Facebook (and similarly) Twitter can now be launched by tapping or clicking their respective tiles on the Start Screen, as shown in the extract below.

Joining Facebook

Signing up to Facebook requires you to be at least 13 years of age, with a computer online to the Internet and a valid e-mail address. Enter **www.facebook.com** into the address bar of Internet Explorer, as shown below and discussed in Chapter 6.

https://www.facebook.com/   ✕   ⊙→

The Facebook **Sign Up** screen appears as shown below.

facebook

Email or Phone   Password
timgatenby@hotmail.com   ••••••••••   Log in
☐ Keep me logged in   Forgotten your password?

Facebook helps you connect and share with the people in your life.

Sign Up
It's free and always will be.

First Name   Last Name

Your email address

Re-enter email address

New Password

Birthday
Day ▾ Month ▾ Year ▾   Why do I need to provide my date of birth?

○ Female   ○ Male

By clicking Sign Up, you agree to our **Terms** and that you have read our **Data Use Policy**, including our **Cookie Use**.

Sign Up

From your e-mail address, Facebook checks your e-mail contacts for people who are already on Facebook. You can then invite them to be Facebook friends. Any e-mail contacts who are not members of Facebook may be sent an invitation to join.

facebook   Search   🔍

Step 1   Step 2   Step 3
Find friends   Profile information Profile picture

Are your friends already on Facebook?
Many of your friends may already be here. Searching your email account is the fastest way to find your friends on Facebook.

✉ **Windows Live Hotmail**

Your Email   timgatenby@hotmail.co.uk

Find friends

Your Facebook Profile or Timeline

You are then asked to start entering your *Profile* information, also called your *Timeline*. The profile or timeline contains details such as your education, employment history, hobbies and interests and your address and contact details

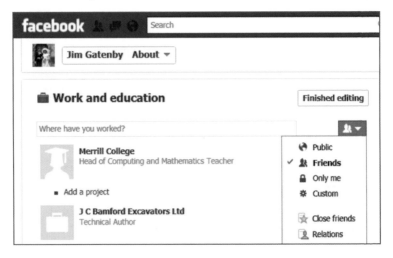

You can also add a profile picture, allowing friends to identify you after a search on Facebook, which may have produced a lot of people with the same name as you. If you have a suitable profile picture stored on your computer, it can be uploaded to Facebook, after clicking **Upload a photo**. Otherwise, if you have a *webcam* on your computer, you can take a picture and upload it directly to Facebook using **Take a photo**.

The Audience Selector

At the right of the slots for some of the personal information you enter is the *inline audience selector* icon, shown on the right. Tap or click this icon to open
the menu shown above on the right. This allows you to control the audience who can view the information, e.g. **Public**, **Friends** and **Only me**, etc.

Posting a Status Update

You can type text messages and add photos in the **Status** box shown below and **Post** updates to a "noticeboard" known as your **Wall**. Others can view your **Wall**, if the privacy settings allow, such as **Public** or **Friends**, as shown on the menu below.

The Facebook App (Windows 8.1 Only)

This is an app in the Windows Store, designed for Windows 8.1. If you try to install the Facebook app in Windows 8, you're told that you need to upgrade your computer to Windows 8.1.

In Windows 8.1, open the Windows Store, and install the Facebook app, using the methods discussed on pages 72-74. This places a tile on the Start Screen, as shown on the right.

As with the Web version, the Facebook app, shown above, has the same main features such as the **Timeline** or **Profile** and the **Status** window for posting updates or news to your Friends.

Introducing Twitter

The Twitter social network has over 200 million *active* users worldwide with many more *registered.* Although there are some similarities with Facebook, Twitter is also different in many ways.

What is a Tweet?

One of the main features of Twitter is that messages or *tweets* can be no more than 140 characters long. This makes Twitter suitable for brief text messages like SMS phone texts. As well as desktop, laptop and tablets computers, Twitter can be used on smartphones such as the iPhone and the Samsung Galaxy.

Whereas e-mails are sent to the unique e-mail addresses of known contacts, tweets can be read by very large numbers of people who may be complete strangers to the tweeter. Twitter is based on the idea that users will want to follow the regular postings of other people such as friends, family, celebrities, politicians, reporters or companies and other organisations.

Followers on Twitter

Regular tweeters may post messages several times a day, such as the actor and writer Stephen Fry, who has millions of *followers*. Some users of Twitter will be followers who only read the tweets of others, rather than posting their own. You need to be sufficiently well-known for lots of other people to want to read what you have to say in your tweets, or find ways of encouraging people to become your followers.

You can choose to follow anyone you like on Twitter, but you can't choose who follows you. You can read all the tweets of the people you follow and send a reply if you wish.

You may also be interested in our book Social Networking for the Older Generation (ISBN 9780859347341) from Bernard Babani (publishing) Ltd.

Using Twitter from the Web Site

You can launch Twitter by logging on to **www.twitter.com**, in a similar way to logging on to Facebook as discussed on page 94.

The Twitter Icons

These icons appear on the Twitter Web page and on the Twitter app, discussed on page 104. Their functions are as follows:

Displays your Timeline, listing all the tweets you've posted.

Lists all the people who've interacted with you, **Favourited** or **Retweeted** your tweet.

Allows you to follow people. Lists tweets with a **Follow** button for you to tap or click.

Shows your biographical details, the number of Tweets you've sent, the number of people you are following and those following you.

The left-hand icon opens a window for you to compose a new Tweet of up to 140 characters. The right-hand icon allows you to search for people to **Follow**.

Signing up for Twitter

Fill in the box, shown below, including a valid e-mail address and a password. Then tap or click **Sign up for Twitter**, as shown below. Your username, for example **@samueljohnson**, and your Twitter account are then created.

Then the **Twitter Teacher** gets you started by providing a list of people for you to follow. When you click the **Follow** button against a person's name and picture, their messages appear on your tweet page. You can also search your e-mail address lists for people to follow on Twitter.

An image of yourself can be added together with a short text profile. An e-mail is sent to you by Twitter and you tap or click a link for confirmation.

Hashtags

A hashtag is a word or phrase, etc., preceded by the hash sign (**#**) and placed in a tweet, e.g. **#BBCQT**. (BBC Question Time). Clicking on a hashtag which appears in a tweet allows you to read all the tweets on that particular topic. You can also find all the relevant tweets by entering the hashtag in the search bar at the top of the Twitter screen as shown below.

Hashtags allow anyone on Twitter to participate in online forums on current news issues or television programs, for example.

Twitter in Use

Whereas Facebook relies heavily on detailed personal profiles to bring together people sharing similar backgrounds and interests, Twitter only accepts about a paragraph of biographical information, as shown below under **findmypast.co.uk**.

Many companies, such as the family history Web site, **findmypast.co.uk**, include a link to Twitter on their main Web site. Clicking this link opens the Twitter Home page of **findmypast.co.uk** as shown below.

Posting a Tweet

Type your message in the box under **What's happening**. The number **99** shown on the lower right below is the number of characters still available to be used out of the maximum of 140. (You don't have to use all 140 characters). To add a photo (up to 3MB) select the camera icon then either browse for a photo or take a photo if you have a camera connected to your computer.

twitter   Search   🔍   **Home** · Profile   Mess

What's happening?

What cid we do before Twitter came along?

📷   99   Tweet

Timeline   @jimgatenby   Activity   Searches   Lists

Click the **Tweet** button shown above to post the tweet.

Reading Tweets

The message is posted and is immediately available on the *timeline* or list of tweets of anyone following you, as shown below. This shows a tweet posted one minute previously by me to anyone following me. My username **@jimgatenby** is shown below. In this case the follower is Christopher Walls, username **@christowalls** — the change in spelling was needed because the full name was already taken by another Twitter user.

Timeline   @christowalls   Activity   Searches ˅   Lists ˅

jimgatenby james gatenby   ›
What did we do before Twitter came along?
1 minute ago ☆ Favorite ⫚ Retweet ↰ Reply

Responding to a Tweet

Shown below is a tweet displayed in the Twitter app.

Clicking or tapping anywhere in the main text expands the tweet and displays the reply options as shown below. The blue text pic.twitter.com/neO2biSG48 is a *link*, automatically created when a photograph is uploaded to Twitter. Tapping or clicking the link opens the photograph, filling the screen.

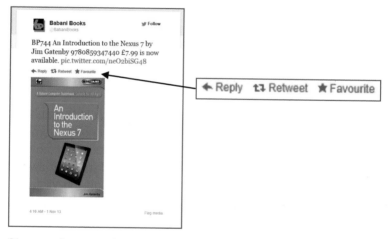

Shown above and below are the options for responding to a tweet.

- **Reply** opens a window for you to post a reply.
- **Retweet** (forward) the tweet to all of your followers.
- **Favourite** makes a list of tweets you like and lets a tweeter know you liked their tweet.

Using the Twitter App

The Windows Store includes a Twitter app, compatible with all versions of Windows 8 and 8.1. Open the Windows Store by tapping or clicking its tile on the

> **Twitter**
> Free ★★★★ 1,523
> Social

Start Screen, as shown on the right. Search or scroll to display the tile for Twitter shown above then tap or click **Install**. A tile for Twitter, as shown below on the right, is soon placed on the Start Screen. Tap the tile to open the Twitter app, as shown below. The layout of the icons on the app screen is different from the Web version of Twitter, but the icons and their functions are the same, as shown below and on page 99.

The Twitter App Home Page

After tapping or clicking the tile for the Twitter app on the Start Screen, the Home Page opens as shown below.

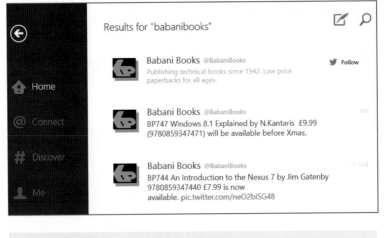

Results for "babanibooks"

Home

Babani Books @BabaniBooks   ▼ **Follow**
Publishing technical books since 1942. Low price paperbacks for all ages.

Connect

Babani Books @BabaniBooks   6d
BP747 Windows 8.1 Explained by N.Kantaris £9.99 (9780859347471) will be available before Xmas.

Discover

Babani Books @BabaniBooks   13d

Me
BP744 An Introduction to the Nexus 7 by Jim Gatenby 9780859347440 £7.99 is now available. pic.twitter.com/neO2biSG48

The Twitter app is compatible with all versions of Windows 8 and 8.1, including Windows RT and Windows RT 8.1

Skype

This is an Internet service which allows you to make free voice and video calls between computers. For example, you could see and speak to friends or relatives in New Zealand in real time without running up a phone bill. All you (both) need is a computer connected to the Internet, equipped with a microphone and speakers. To see each other in a video call you also need a webcam on each machine. The latest tablet and laptop computers have all these accessories built-in from new. If necessary, especially on desktop machines, these devices can be bought separately for a few pounds and simply plugged in, ready to use straightaway.

There is a Skype app for Windows 8 and 8.1, available from the Windows Store. This is free and can be downloaded after tapping or clicking the Store tile on the Start Screen shown on the right.

Then scroll across the Store and tap or click the **Skype** tile shown on the right. This opens the description window shown below including an **Install** button. When you select the **Install** button a tile for launching Skype is placed on the Start Screen of the Modern UI.

Creating a New Skype Name and Password

The e-mail names and addresses in your People feature as discussed earlier are used as your Skype contacts list. You are signed in to Skype automatically using the e-mail address and password for your Microsoft account. To create a new Skype account you need to set up a new Microsoft User account in **Change PC settings**, on the **Settings** charm, as discussed on page 81. Skype opens with a list of your contacts. Tap or click the required contact to see if they're **available**, as shown on the right in the blue area. Tap or click the left-hand icon to make a video call using a webcam or select the middle icon to make a voice only call. Tap or click the right-hand plus icon above to allow others to join the conversation. After you tap or click to make a call, your contact (if online), will hear the dial tone and can tap or click their green phone icon to accept the call.

If your contact is not online when you call, you can use Skype on your computer to call a mobile phone or landline. Unlike calls between two computers on the Internet, there is a charge for these calls, for which you need credit in your Skype account.

During a video call, the participants should be visible to each other and the following icons are displayed:

These icons represent a webcam (video call), microphone (mute/unmute), instant messaging and the red icon used to end a call.

Software Compatibility

Introduction

This chapter discusses the two main types of software on any computer:

- The Operating System
- The Applications Software or Apps

The operating system is a collection of software which controls the basic functions of the computer, no matter what activity you have chosen to do.

The applications software consists of the programs or apps which perform your chosen activities, such as word processing a document, editing a photograph or playing a game.

The Windows Operating System

At the time of writing the Windows 8.1 operating system has just been released and Windows 8 is still available. A free upgrade from Windows 8 to Windows 8.1 can be downloaded from the Windows Store, as discussed on page 110. In the same way Windows RT can be upgraded to Windows RT 8.1.

Computers running Windows XP, Vista or Windows 7 can be upgraded to Windows 8 or 8.1 either by a download from **windows.microsoft.com** or by purchasing a DVD package.

It may be cheaper for users of Windows XP, Vista or Windows 7 to upgrade first to Windows 8, then use the free upgrade from the Windows Store to install Windows 8.1.

In general, notes in this chapter for Windows 8.1 also apply to Windows 8, Windows RT and Windows RT 8.1, unless otherwise stated.

Upgrading Windows XP or Vista

To check whether your computer can run Windows 8.1, download and run the free *Windows 8.1 Upgrade Assistant* at **windows.microsoft.com**. The minimum specification for a computer to run Windows 8.1 is shown in the following table.

Minimum System Requirements

	32-bit	64-bit
Processor speed: gigahertz	1GHz	1GHz
RAM: Main memory gigabytes	1GB	2GB
Hard disc drive, free space	16GB	20GB
DirectX 9 graphics card with WDDM driver		

To upgrade Windows XP or Vista, you can buy a package containing two Windows 8.1 DVDs, designated *32-bit* and *64-bit*. The 64-bit version works faster but not all computers can run it. To find out if your computer can use the 64-bit version, select **Control Panel**, **System and Security**, **System**, **Performance Information and Tools** and **View and print detailed performance system and information**. It should say "**64-bit capable Yes**" if your computer can run the 64-bit version. If in doubt you are advised to install the 32-bit version initially.

The Clean Install

When upgrading from Windows XP or Windows Vista, the hard disc drive is wiped or *formatted* in a *clean install*. So before installing Windows 8.1 from a DVD, you need to back up any important data files. Insert the Windows 8.1 DVD in the drive, then follow the instructions on the screen. You will need to enter the 25-character product key. During the installation the computer will restart several times. After installing Windows 8.1 you will need to reinstall your application software.

Upgrading Windows 7

Windows 7 can be upgraded to Windows 8.1 by *downloading* the software from the Internet, after first downloading the *Upgrade Assistant* to check that your computer system is compatible. You can also choose to keep your personal files. Locate the DVDs for any apps you may wish to re-install after Windows 8.1 has been installed, then log on to **windows.microsoft.com** and select **Downloads**.

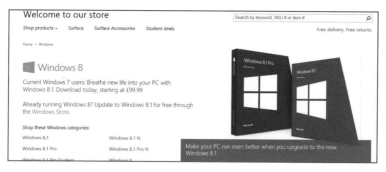

You can then choose the version of Windows 8.1 to buy and place your order for the download and a backup CD if you wish. Then enter your name, address and bank card details. A receipt is then e-mailed to you, together with your Windows 8.1 *product code*. During the upgrade process the product code is entered automatically. However the code should be kept safe as it will be needed if you ever have to reinstall Windows 8.1.

Tap or click **Next** to download Windows 8.1. The time for the download depends on the speed of your Internet connection but can vary between 30 minutes and 3 hours. After downloading Windows 8.1, tap or click **Install now** (recommended) to start upgrading your computer. Alternatively, you can create a Windows 8.1 file on a blank DVD or flash drive for installation later, perhaps on a different computer.

You can buy a DVD and carry out a clean install to upgrade Windows 7 to Windows 8.1, as discussed on page 108.

Upgrading Windows 8 to Windows 8.1

Windows 8 can be upgraded to Windows 8.1 using the Windows Store. (Windows RT can be upgraded to Windows RT 8.1 in the same way). Open the Windows Store by tapping the tile on the Start Screen, as discussed on page 72. You should see the **Update Windows** panel in the Windows Store, as shown below.

If the **Update Windows** panel doesn't appear in your Windows Store, as shown on the right, this may be because Windows 8 or RT has not been kept up-to-date with the latest "patches". Patches are regular small updates downloaded to your computer to add new features or improve security. (These

small patch updates are not to be confused with the major update to convert Windows 8 to Windows 8.1.) To check that Windows 8 or RT is up-to-date, open the **Control Panel**, as discussed on page 48, then select **System and Security** and **Windows Update**. Make sure the latest Windows 8 or RT automatic patches have been installed. Then you should see the **Update Windows** panel in the Windows Store, as shown above.

Tap or click **Update to Windows 8.1 for free**, shown above, then tap or click **Download** to begin the installation of Windows 8.1 or Windows RT 8.1. The time taken for the upgrade will depend on the speed of your Internet connection, but could take a few hours. During the upgrade the computer will restart a few times.

Your personal files created in Windows 8 or RT and any Windows Desktop apps you installed will still be available in Windows 8.1 or RT 8.1. However, you may need to re-install some of the Modern User Interface apps you had previously downloaded from the Windows Store.

Applications Software for Windows 8.1

Windows 8.1 can run apps (or programs) from the sources shown below. (Notes for Windows 8.1 also apply to Windows 8.)

- Apps pre-installed as part of Windows 8.1 with tiles on the Start Screen.

- Apps downloaded from the Windows Store, with tiles on the Start Screen.

- Apps designed for earlier versions of Windows such as Windows 7. These run in the Windows Desktop but can have tiles pinned to the Windows 8.1 Start Screen.

Windows 8.1 runs on computers with *x64* and *x86* processors, making them compatible with traditional business software such as Microsoft Office, used on millions of computers throughout the world. Windows RT and RT 8.1 cannot run traditional Windows software — apps must be specially written for RT and RT 8.1.

Installing Traditional Windows Software

As an example, I describe below the installation of Microsoft Publisher, part of the Microsoft Office suite of software. Publisher is widely used on computers running Windows XP and Windows 7 and can be installed on computers running Windows 8.1 (but not RT and RT 8.1), as described below.

With the Windows 8.1 Start Screen displayed, insert the Microsoft Publisher DVD. A message appears in the top right-hand corner of the screen, as shown below.

DVD RW Drive (F:) OFFICE14
Tap to choose what happens with this disc.

Tap or click in the message area then select **Run SETUP.EXE** from the menu which pops up. Next you are asked to enter your 25-character Product Key. This is normally found on a label on the packaging for the software.

The installation of the software is now automatic and should only take a few minutes, after which you need to restart the computer to complete the process.

Microsoft Publisher should appear on the Apps screen as shown on the right. Opening the Apps screen  is discussed on page 7. Briefly hold then swipe the app up or down, or right click with a mouse, to display the following toolbar across the bottom of the screen.

Then tap or click **Pin to Start**, shown above, to place a tile for Publisher on the Start Screen. The toolbar shown above can also be used to **Uninstall** programs or apps that are no longer required. Tap the new tile to open Publisher in the traditional Desktop with the Ribbon across the top and the Taskbar along the bottom, as shown below.

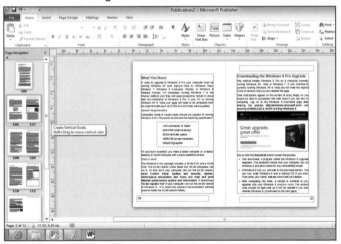

Applications Software for Windows RT 8.1

Windows RT 8.1 runs on tablet computers which use the ARM processor. These computers can't generally run traditional software designed for Windows XP and Windows 7. The sources of software for Windows RT 8.1 are:

- Apps having tiles on the Start Screen of a new computer on which Windows RT 8.1 is pre-installed.

- These include special versions of Microsoft Office, i.e. Word, Excel, PowerPoint and OneNote, which have been converted to run on Windows RT 8.1.

- Apps downloaded from the Windows Store using Windows RT 8.1 and pinned to the Start Screen.

Apps installed as tiles on the Start Screen by default and apps from the Windows Store were discussed earlier in this book. The next section outlines the Office 2013 software which is included with Windows RT 8.1. The four apps appear as tiles on the Start Screen of a new RT 8.1 tablet as shown below. These apps are Word 2013, Excel 2013, PowerPoint 2013 and OneNote 2013, converted to run on Windows RT 8.1.

Microsoft Word is probably the world's most popular word processing program, used for producing anything from a simple letter, to a report or thesis or a complete book such as this one.

Microsoft Excel is a popular spreadsheet program, used for automating the calculation of tables of numbers in accounts and scientific work, including the production of graphs and charts.

PowerPoint is used to make presentations to audiences such as clubs, business meetings or family gatherings. Screens include text and photographs and can be presented in a slide show.

OneNote is a program designed to collect all of your information from different sources and organise it into an easily retrievable single system. Information may include typed notes, Web addresses, Web pages, photos and video clips, for example.

When you tap or click the tile for one of the Office 2013 RT 8.1 apps such as Word 2013, the program opens in the traditional Windows Desktop, as shown on the right. The Taskbar along the bottom has icons for OneNote, PowerPoint, Word and Excel, as shown below.

Along the top of the Word page shown below is the Office Ribbon, with icons for all the word processing tasks such as page layout, formatting text and saving and printing.

Glossary of Terms

App

A program or application designed for a specific purpose such as accounts, a game, playing music or desktop publishing.

ARM Processor

A design of processor used in tablet computers and mobile phones. Its low power consumption increases battery life in mobile devices.

Charms

A set of icons on the right of the screen. Used for settings, searching the computer, returning to the Start Screen, etc.

Control Panel

A feature which provides access to all of the settings on the computer such as security, screen display and personalization.

Desktop

The main screen used on earlier versions of Windows and included in Windows 8.1 to run traditional Windows applications.

Gestures

Finger movements used to control a touchscreen computer.

Lock Screen

The startup screen. May require a password to proceed.

Metro

The original name for the Modern UI.

Modern UI

The user interface operated by touchscreen or mouse and keyboard, includes Start Screen, Lock Screen, All apps.

Notification

Brief updates on the screen, e.g. informing you of new e-mails, etc.

Operating System

Software such as Windows 8.1 used to control the computer, irrespective of what apps are running.

Processor

Microchips which execute programs. The processor is often referred to as the "brains" of the computer.

Program

A set of instructions written in a special language or code, used to control the computer. Also known as an app or application.

Start Screen

An array of tiles on the screen used to launch apps and Web pages.

Tablet

A hand-held, battery-powered, touchscreen computer such as the Microsoft Surface, Apple iPad, Nexus 7 or Samsung Galaxy.

Tiles

Small rectangular panels on the Start Screen used to launch apps and Web sites. Live tiles display constantly changing information.

Touchscreen

A screen used to control a computer using finger gestures.

Windows 8.1

The basic version of the operating system, installed by computer builders, also known as OEM (Original Equipment Manufacturers).

Windows 8.1 Pro

The retail version of Windows 8.1, sold as a download or DVD for upgrading a computer, e.g. from Windows XP, Vista or Windows 7.

Windows RT 8.1

Special versions of Windows 8.1 for ARM tablet computers.

Windows Store

An online collection of thousands of apps. Apps are either free or can be purchased before downloading to Windows 8.1 or RT 8.1.

x64 and x86

Types of processor used in PC computers running Windows XP, Vista , Windows 7 and Windows 8.1 (but not Windows RT 8.1)

Index

A

Address Bar 53, 63, 67
Apps screen 3, 7, 48
Apps 1, 12-14
   downloading...................73
   launching 18, 20
   multi-tasking...................22
   show Apps not Start........9
   switching 21
ARM processor 2, 113,115
Attachment 79, 83, 86

B

bing 53, 63, 64
Broadband 49
   mobile 51
   speed 59, 60

C

Charms Bar...................23, 25
Computer, shutting down ...26
Control Panel .. 14, 27, 34, 48

D

Desktop...........................8, 9
   background 34
   start computer in 9

E

Ease of Access   26, 29, 39-48
Electronic mail 79-90
   App...............................80
E-mail address 81
Emoticon 85

F

Facebook 93-97
Fibre optic 52, 59
FTTC 59
FTTH 59

G

Gestures 17
Google 63, 66

H

High Contrast 39, 43
Hyperlink............................ 68

I

Internet...........................63-78
   Access Point............50, 54
   adaptor 50
   Explorer 18, 53
   security 75
   Service Provider 52
   speed 59

K

Keyboard shortcuts 28

L

Link, hyperlink 68
Lock Screen............15, 30, 33

M

Magnifier 39, 41
Mail App 13, 80
Malware 75
Microsoft Surface.................6
Modern User Interface .3, 115

Mouse operations 16
Multi-tasking 22

N
Narrator 39, 42

O
Office software suite . 111, 113
On-Screen Keyboard 39, 43
Operating system 1, 107

P
People App 13, 92
Personalising 26, 29-38
Picture, account 32, 33
Printer, connecting 61
Processor 4, 115, 116

R
Router 50, 54, 56

S
Screen resolution 29, 38
Search engine 63, 66
Searching 23, 24, 64-66
Security 51, 75
Settings charm 25, 39, 54
SkyDrive 14, 89
Skype 105
Sleep Mode 27
Social Networking 91-106
Software (applications)
Windows 8.1 111
Windows RT 8.1 113
Speech Recognition 39, 45
Start button and menu .. 19, 48
Start Screen . 3, 10, 18, 19, 31

T
Tabbed browsing 70
Text size 37
Tiles 10, 18
live 11
Pin to Start 20, 69, 94
Touch gestures 17
Travel App 12
Twitter 98-104

V
Viruses 75

W
Weather App 13
Web address 67
Web browser 50, 53, 63
WiFi 51, 54
Windows 1-14
Defender 78
Firewall 77
SmartScreen 78
Store 71, 110
Update 77
Windows 8.1 3-5
upgrading 108-110
navigating 15-28
requirements 108
RT 8.1 .... 4-6, 113-116
software 111
versions 4, 116
x64, x86 processor 4, 116